MW00960354

THE BEGINNER'S GUIDE TO
PODCASTING
2025

Everything You Need to Know to Launch Your Own Podcast,
Including Choosing a Niche, Selecting Equipment,
Structuring Your Show, and Distributing Your Episodes.

KAREN NOIL

ISBN: 9798338128275

Table of Contents

Introduction

Are you looking for a new and exciting way to share your ideas and connect with others? Look no further than podcasting. With the rise of technology and social media, podcasting has become a powerful tool for storytelling, education, and entertainment. Whether you have a passion for a specific topic or want to showcase your expertise, podcasting allows you to reach a global audience and make your mark in the digital world. In this chapter, we'll explore the power of podcasting, who can benefit from creating their own podcast, and what sets successful podcasts apart.

Unleashing the Power of Podcasting

Podcasting is a phenomenon that has taken the world by storm. With millions of people tuning in to listen to their favorite podcasts every day, it's clear that this medium has a power unlike any other. So what makes podcasting so special? Let's dive in and explore the incredible power of podcasting.

One of the key advantages of podcasting is its accessibility. Unlike traditional forms of media, such as television or radio, podcasts can be consumed anytime, anywhere. Whether you're commuting to work, doing chores around the house, or even just taking a leisurely stroll, you can easily tune in to your favorite podcast with just a few taps on your smartphone. This accessibility means that podcasting has the ability to reach a global audience, breaking down geographical barriers and allowing people from all walks of life to connect and engage with content that interests them.

Another powerful aspect of podcasting is its ability to foster deep connections. Listening to a podcast feels personal and intimate, like having a one-on-one conversation with the host. This sense of intimacy can create a unique bond between the listener and the podcast, leading to a dedicated and loyal audience. As a podcast creator, this can be incredibly rewarding, as you have the opportunity to form genuine connections with your listeners and build a community around your content.

Podcasting is also a fantastic tool for storytelling. Whether you're sharing personal experiences, interviewing guests, or discussing a particular topic, podcasts allow for in-depth conversations and storytelling that can captivate and engage listeners. The audio format allows for nuance and emotion to be conveyed in a way that is often lost in written or visual media. With podcasting, you have the power to transport your listeners to new worlds, spark their imagination, and leave a lasting impact.

Lastly, podcasting offers immense creative freedom. Unlike traditional media outlets, podcasts are not subject to the same limitations and regulations. You have complete control over your content, allowing you to express yourself fully and explore topics that may not be covered in mainstream media. This freedom allows for innovation and experimentation, making podcasting an exciting and dynamic medium to be a part of.

Determining If Podcasting is Right for You

Are you considering starting your own podcast? It's important to take a moment and determine if podcasting is the right fit for you. While podcasting can be a rewarding and exciting journey, it does require a certain level of commitment and dedication. In this section, we'll explore some key factors to consider when deciding if podcasting is right for you.

First and foremost, it's important to think about your passion and expertise. What are you truly passionate about? What knowledge or experiences do you have to share? Podcasting is most successful when you have a genuine interest in the topic you'll be discussing. It's this passion that will drive your episodes and keep your listeners engaged. So take some time to reflect on your interests and determine if there's a topic that you're truly passionate about and eager to dive into.

Next, consider your available time and resources. Podcasting requires a commitment of time and energy. From planning and researching episodes to recording and editing, there's a significant amount of work involved in creating a podcast. So it's important to assess if you have the time and resources available to dedicate to this endeavor. Think about your current schedule and responsibilities and determine if you can realistically fit podcasting into your routine. It may be helpful to create a rough outline of the tasks involved in podcasting and estimate how much time you would need to allocate to each one.

Another factor to consider is your ability to engage with an audience. Podcasting is all about building a connection with your listeners and engaging them with your content. Are you comfortable speaking in front of a microphone? Do you enjoy communicating your ideas and thoughts to others? These are important questions to ask yourself because podcasting requires a certain level of confidence and charisma to captivate your audience. If you're someone who enjoys speaking and has a natural ability to engage others, podcasting might be a great fit for you.

Lastly, consider the long-term commitment involved in podcasting. Building a successful podcast takes time and consistency. It's not an overnight success, but rather a journey that requires ongoing dedication. So before diving in, ask yourself if you're willing to commit to podcasting in the long run. Are you willing to consistently produce episodes, engage with your audience, and continuously improve your podcasting skills?

In conclusion, determining if podcasting is right for you involves assessing your passion, available time and resources, ability to engage with an audience, and long-term commitment.

1 Podcasting 101: A Beginner's Guide to This Engaging Medium

Podcasting has become a popular form of media in recent years, with millions of people tuning in to their favorite shows and episodes every day. But what exactly is podcasting? In simple terms, it is a type of digital audio file that can be downloaded or streamed online. Think of it as a radio show that you can listen to on demand. However, what sets podcasting apart is its diverse range of content and the ability for anyone to create and share their own show. In this beginner's guide, we will delve into the world of podcasting, exploring its history, current landscape, and why it has become such an engaging medium for listeners and creators alike. Whether you are new to podcasting or looking to learn more about this growing industry, this book is the perfect place to start.

What Exactly is a Podcast?

Podcasting has taken the world by storm in recent years, but what exactly is a podcast? Simply put, a podcast is a digital audio file that can be downloaded or streamed online. It's like a radio show that you can listen to whenever and wherever you want. Unlike traditional radio, podcasts offer a diverse range of content, covering topics as broad as true crime, history, comedy, news, and self-help. With thousands of shows to choose from, there's something for everyone in the podcasting world.

The term "podcast" is a combination of "iPod" (remember those?) and "broadcast." The name reflects the medium's roots, as early podcasting was designed for playback on portable media devices like the iPod. However, with the rise of smartphones and streaming services, you can now access podcasts on virtually any device with an internet connection.

One of the key aspects of podcasting is its accessibility. Anyone can create and share their own podcast. All you need is a microphone, recording software, and a platform to host your episodes. This democratic nature of podcasting has given rise to an explosion of independent creators, who are not bound by the restrictions of traditional media. It has allowed marginalized voices and niche interests to find their audience, making podcasting a truly inclusive and diverse medium.

Podcasts can be scripted or unscripted, with some hosts conducting interviews, while others simply share their thoughts and experiences. They can range from just a few minutes to several hours in length, providing options for listeners with varying preferences. Podcasts often have a conversational tone, creating a sense of intimacy and connection between the host and the audience. It's like having a personal conversation with someone, even if you're just listening to their show.

One of the advantages of podcasting is the ability to

consume content on demand. Unlike traditional radio or television, podcasts are not bound by time slots. You can listen to them whenever and wherever you want, making it a convenient form of entertainment for people with busy schedules. Whether you're commuting to work, doing chores around the house, or going for a run, podcasts can accompany you and make the time fly by.

Another great feature of podcasts is the ability to subscribe to your favorite shows. Subscribing ensures that you never miss an episode. When a new episode is released, it is automatically downloaded to your device or added to your streaming queue. This makes it easy to stay up to date with your favorite shows without having to manually search for new episodes every time.

As the podcasting industry has grown, so too has the range of topics and genres available. Whether you're into true crime, sports, history, comedy, or even niche hobbies, there is a podcast out there for you. With so many options, it can be overwhelming to navigate the podcasting landscape. However, the sheer variety of content ensures that there is always something new and interesting to discover.

Podcasts have also become a popular medium for storytelling. From investigative journalism to serialized fiction, podcasts have the ability to captivate and engage listeners like no other medium. Many podcasts are known for their immersive storytelling techniques, creating an audio experience that draws listeners in and keeps them hooked episode after episode. With high production values and talented storytellers, podcasts have become an art form in their own right.

In addition to entertainment, podcasts can also be a valuable source of information and education. Many podcasts feature experts in various fields, who share their knowledge and insights with listeners. Whether you want to learn about personal finance, psychology, science, or history, there is a podcast that can satisfy your intellectual curiosity. Podcasts offer a unique blend of entertainment and education, making them a perfect medium for lifelong learners.

The Current State of the Podcasting Landscape

Over the past few years, podcasting has exploded in popularity and has firmly established itself as a major form of media. With millions of podcasts available and millions of listeners tuning in regularly, it's safe to say that the podcasting landscape is thriving.

One of the most noticeable trends in the current state of podcasting is the sheer variety of content available. No matter what your interests are, there is a podcast out there for you. From true crime and comedy to history and self-help, podcasts cover a wide range of topics and genres. This diversity of content has contributed to the widespread appeal of podcasting, as listeners can find shows that cater to their specific interests and preferences.

Another significant aspect of the podcasting landscape is the emergence of high-quality productions. Gone are the days when podcasts were simply recorded conversations between friends. Now, many podcasts feature professional-grade audio, immersive storytelling techniques, and top-notch production values. This level of quality has elevated podcasting to a new level and has attracted listeners who appreciate well-crafted content.

In addition to the variety and quality of podcasts, the accessibility of the medium has also contributed to its popularity. Unlike traditional forms of media, podcasts can be listened to at any time and from anywhere. With the rise of smartphones and streaming platforms, podcasts can be easily accessed on the go. This convenience factor has made podcasting a go-to choice for people with busy lifestyles who want to consume entertainment or gain knowledge while on the move.

One of the most significant indicators of the podcasting landscape's growth is the increase in listenership and audience engagement. According to recent surveys, the number of podcast listeners continues to rise year after year. This upward trend shows that podcasts have become a preferred form of entertainment for many people. Additionally, podcasts have developed a loyal following, with listeners eagerly anticipating new episodes and actively engaging with hosts and other listeners through social media and online communities.

The growth of podcasting has also resulted in the emergence of podcast networks and partnerships. As the medium has become more established, major media companies and celebrities have entered the podcasting space, bringing their resources and star power with them. This has led to collaborations between traditional media outlets and podcast creators, as well as the creation of exclusive content for specific platforms or networks. These developments have further propelled the podcasting industry forward and opened up new opportunities for creators and listeners alike.

Another important aspect of the podcasting landscape is the monetization of podcasts. While many podcasts are still independently produced and distributed for free, there has been a significant increase in advertising and sponsorship opportunities. As podcasts attract larger audiences, advertisers have recognized the potential reach and engagement of the medium. This has led to partnerships between podcasters and brands, with podcast hosts endorsing products or featuring advertisements within their episodes. Monetization has provided podcast creators with the opportunity to turn their passion into a profitable venture and has fueled further growth in the industry.

The future of the podcasting landscape looks

promising. As the medium continues to gain popularity and attract new listeners, we can expect to see further innovation and diversification of content. New technologies, such as smart speakers and voice assistants, are also shaping the future of podcasting by providing more convenient ways to listen and discover new shows. Additionally, as podcasting becomes more mainstream, we can anticipate continued growth in advertising revenue and investment in the industry.

2 Interest to Income: How to Find Your Podcasting Niche

Have you been thinking about starting a podcast but don't know where to begin? Are you passionate about a certain topic but unsure if it would make a successful podcast? Finding your niche is an essential step in creating a successful and sustainable podcast. It not only helps you stay motivated and engaged, but it also attracts and retains listeners. In this chapter, we will discuss the process of finding your podcasting niche by identifying your passion and expertise, as well as researching and understanding your audience. By the end, you'll be on your way to turning your interest into income through podcasting.

Understanding the Concept of a Podcasting Niche

When it comes to podcasting, having a clear understanding of the concept of a niche is crucial. A podcasting niche refers to a specific topic or theme that your podcast revolves around. It is what sets your podcast apart from others and attracts a specific audience. Understanding the concept of a podcasting niche will help you create content that resonates with your target audience and ultimately leads to a successful podcasting journey.

First and foremost, a podcasting niche allows you to narrow down your focus and cater to a specific group of listeners who share a common interest. Instead of trying to appeal to a broad audience, having a niche helps you to establish yourself as an expert in a particular field. For example, if you're passionate about personal finance, your podcasting niche could be centered around providing financial advice, tips for saving money, and stories of successful financial journeys. By focusing on this niche, you can attract listeners who are specifically interested in personal finance and increase the chances of building a dedicated fan base.

In addition to narrowing down your focus, having a niche also allows you to create unique and valuable content. When you have a specific topic or theme, you can dive deeper into it, providing in-depth discussions and insights that are relevant to your audience. This level of specialization and expertise sets you apart from other general podcasts and gives your audience a reason to tune in to your show. By delivering valuable content that meets the needs and interests of your target audience, you build credibility and trust, which are vital for the long-term success of your podcast.

Another benefit of understanding the concept of a podcasting niche is that it helps you stand out in a saturated market. With thousands of podcasts available, finding a unique angle or perspective within your niche can be challenging but rewarding. By identifying a specific aspect or angle that sets your podcast apart from others, you increase the chances of attracting listeners who are looking for something different. Whether it's a specific storytelling style, a unique format, or an underrepresented perspective, finding your niche within a broader topic will help you differentiate yourself in a crowded podcasting landscape.

Moreover, a well-defined podcasting niche allows you to connect with your audience on a deeper level. When you cater to a specific group of people who share a common interest, you can create a sense of community and engage in meaningful conversations. By understanding your audience's needs, desires, and pain points, you can tailor your content to address their specific concerns and provide solutions. This personalized approach not only strengthens the connection with your listeners but also encourages them to become loyal fans who eagerly await each new episode.

How to Identify and Harness Your Unique Passion and Expertise for Podcasting

When it comes to finding your podcasting niche, the first step is to identify your unique passion and expertise. Your passion is what fuels your excitement and dedication to your podcast, while your expertise is what sets you apart as an authority in your chosen field. By combining these two elements, you can create content that is both authentic and valuable to your audience.

To begin identifying your passion, ask yourself what topics or activities excite you the most. Think about the things that you could talk about for hours on end, without ever getting tired. This could be a hobby, a profession, or even a personal interest. The key is to choose a topic that you genuinely enjoy and have a deep knowledge or experience in.

Next, consider your expertise. What skills or knowledge do you possess that others may find valuable? This could be based on your education, professional background, or personal experiences. Think about what unique insights or perspectives you can offer to your audience. For example, if you have a background in marketing, you could create a podcast focused on providing marketing strategies and tips for small businesses.

Once you have identified your passion and expertise, it's important to find a way to connect them. Look for areas where your passion and expertise intersect, as this will be the sweet spot for your podcasting niche. This is where you will have the most to offer and where you will be most motivated to create content.

For example, if you are passionate about fitness and have expertise in nutrition, your podcasting niche could be centered around providing fitness tips and advice, while also diving deep into the science behind nutrition and how it relates to overall health. By combining your passion for fitness with your expertise in nutrition, you can create a podcast that is both enjoyable for you to create and valuable for your listeners.

Another way to identify your unique passion and expertise is to ask yourself what problems you are uniquely positioned to solve. Consider the challenges that your target audience may be facing and how your passion and expertise can help address them. By understanding the needs and pain points of your audience, you can create content that is highly relevant and helpful.

In addition to identifying your passion and expertise, it's important to continually harness and refine them. Keep learning and staying up to date with the latest trends and developments in your chosen field. Attend workshops, conferences, or webinars related to your passion and expertise to deepen your knowledge and expand your network. This will not only help you create better content but also position yourself as a trusted authority in your niche.

Remember, finding your podcasting niche is a process that takes time and exploration. Be open to experimenting with different topics and formats until you find what resonates with you and your audience. Your passion and expertise are the foundation for a successful podcast, so invest the time and effort to identify and harness them. In doing so, you will not only create a podcast that you love but also attract and retain loyal listeners who share your enthusiasm and interest.

Effective Techniques for Researching and Understanding Your Potential Audience

To create a successful podcast, it's important to research and understand your potential audience. This step is crucial for finding your podcasting niche and creating content that resonates with your target listeners. Here are some effective techniques for researching and understanding your potential audience:

1. Define your target audience: Start by identifying who your ideal listeners are. Consider factors such as age, gender, location, interests, and any other demographics that are relevant to your podcast. Defining your target audience will help you tailor your content and marketing strategies to reach the right people.

2. Conduct surveys and interviews: One of the best ways to understand your potential audience is by directly engaging with them. Conduct surveys or interviews to gather insights about their interests, preferences, and needs. Ask open-ended questions to encourage detailed responses and gain a deeper understanding of what they are looking for in a podcast.

3. Utilize social media platforms: Social media

platforms are valuable tools for understanding your potential audience. Join relevant groups or communities on platforms such as Facebook, X, or Reddit, where your target audience may gather. Pay attention to their discussions, comments, and questions to gain insights into their interests and pain points.

4. Analyze competitor podcasts: Take the time to listen to podcasts that are similar to the niche you're considering. Analyze their content, format, and engagement with their audience. Pay attention to the reviews, comments, and feedback they receive to understand what works well and what can be improved. This analysis will help you identify gaps in the market and opportunities to differentiate your podcast.

5. Use analytics tools: Utilize analytics tools such as Google Analytics, Apple Podcast Analytics, or Podtrac to gather data about your potential audience. These tools can provide valuable insights on listener demographics, geographic location, listening habits, and more. Analyze this data to identify trends and patterns that can inform your content creation and marketing strategies.

6. Engage with your potential audience: Engage with your potential audience through various channels such as social media, email newsletters, or your podcast's website. Respond to their comments and questions,

and encourage them to provide feedback. This two-way communication not only helps you understand their needs and interests better but also builds a sense of community and loyalty.

7. Stay updated with industry trends: Stay updated with industry trends and developments related to your podcasting niche. Subscribe to newsletters, blogs, or podcasts that cover your niche to stay informed. This knowledge will help you understand what your potential audience is currently interested in and adapt your content accordingly.

8. Use keyword research tools: Keyword research tools such as Google Keyword Planner, Ubersuggest, or SEMrush can provide valuable insights into the topics and keywords your potential audience is searching for. Use these tools to identify popular search queries related to your podcasting niche. This will not only help you optimize your content for search engines but also give you a better understanding of what your audience is looking for.

Remember, researching and understanding your potential audience is an ongoing process. Continuously gather feedback, analyze data, and engage with your listeners to ensure that your content remains relevant and valuable to them. By understanding your audience's needs and preferences, you can create a podcast that resonates with them and attracts a dedicated fan base.

Tips and Tricks for Choosing the Perfect Podcasting Niche

So you've identified your passion and expertise, conducted research on your potential audience, and now it's time to choose the perfect podcasting niche. Here are some tips and tricks to help you make that decision:

1. Follow your passion: When choosing a podcasting niche, it's important to select a topic that you are genuinely passionate about. This will not only keep you motivated and excited about creating content but will also come through in your episodes and resonate with your audience. Remember, your passion will shine through in your podcast and make it more enjoyable for both you and your listeners.

2. Consider audience demand: While following your passion is crucial, it's also essential to consider the demand for your chosen niche. Ask yourself if there is a significant audience interested in your topic. Look for communities, forums, or social media groups dedicated to your niche and see if there is active engagement and discussion. This will give you an indication of whether there is a potential audience for your podcast.

3. Identify gaps in the market: While researching competitor podcasts, pay attention to any gaps or opportunities within your chosen niche. Is there something missing or a perspective that hasn't been explored? Identifying these gaps will help you

differentiate your podcast and provide something unique to your audience. By offering a fresh take or providing valuable insights that others have overlooked, you can attract listeners who are looking for something different.

4. Leverage your unique perspective: Think about what makes your perspective unique within your chosen niche. What experiences, skills, or insights do you bring to the table? This could be your professional background, personal experiences, or a combination of both. Leveraging your unique perspective will set you apart from others in the same niche and attract listeners who are interested in your specific viewpoint.

5. Test your ideas: Before fully committing to a podcasting niche, consider testing your ideas with a smaller audience. This could involve creating a few episodes, sharing them with a select group of individuals, and gathering their feedback. This process will help you refine your content and ensure that you're heading in the right direction. Additionally, it allows you to make any necessary adjustments before launching your podcast to a wider audience.

6. Stay adaptable: Remember that choosing a podcasting niche is not set in stone. As you grow and evolve as a podcaster, you may discover new interests, passions, or opportunities. Stay adaptable and open to adjusting your niche if necessary. It's important to find a balance between staying true to your original vision

and being flexible enough to embrace new possibilities.

7. Be consistent: Once you've chosen your podcasting niche, it's essential to maintain consistency in your content and release schedule. Consistency builds trust with your audience and keeps them coming back for more. Establish a regular publishing schedule that works for you and commit to it. This consistency will help you grow your podcast and attract a dedicated following.

Remember, choosing the perfect podcasting niche is a process that requires careful consideration, research, and self-reflection. By following your passion, understanding audience demand, and leveraging your unique perspective, you can find a niche that resonates with you and your potential listeners. Be open to experimentation, stay adaptable, and most importantly, have fun throughout the process.

3 The ABCs of Podcasting: Planning Your Show from A to Z

Are you thinking about starting a podcast but feeling overwhelmed by the planning process? Don't worry, you're not alone. Many aspiring podcasters struggle with defining their concept, structuring their episodes, and coming up with a catchy name. But fear not, because in this chapter, we'll cover the ABCs of podcasting and walk you through the steps of planning your show from A to Z. By the end of this post, you'll have a clear understanding of how to craft a unique and engaging podcast that stands out in the crowded world of podcasting.

Setting the Stage: Defining Your Podcast Concept

When it comes to podcasting, the first and most important step is to define your podcast concept. Your concept is essentially the foundation upon which your entire show will be built. It's what will attract and captivate your audience, making them want to come back for more.

Defining your podcast concept requires you to ask yourself some key questions. What do you want your podcast to be about? What topics or themes are you passionate about? What unique perspective or angle can you bring to these topics? How do you want your audience to feel when they listen to your show?

To get started, think about your own interests and expertise. What are you knowledgeable about or have a deep passion for? Your podcast should be something that excites you, as that enthusiasm will shine through in your episodes. Don't worry about trying to appeal to a broad audience – instead, focus on catering to a specific niche or community that shares your interests.

Next, consider the format and structure of your podcast. Will it be a solo show where you share your thoughts and insights? Or do you envision having guest interviews or panel discussions? Understanding the format will help you determine the length, frequency, and overall flow of your episodes.

Additionally, it's important to think about the target audience for your podcast. Who do you want to reach with your show? Are they beginners in the subject matter or experts? This will influence how you present information and the level of depth you go into during your episodes.

Once you have a clear idea of your podcast concept, it's helpful to create a mission statement or elevator pitch that succinctly captures what your show is all about. This statement will serve as a guiding light throughout the planning and production process, reminding you of your podcast's purpose and helping you stay focused.

Defining your podcast concept is not a one-size-fits-all process. It requires introspection and creativity. Take the time to brainstorm, research, and explore different ideas until you land on a concept that feels right for you. Don't be afraid to think outside the box or challenge conventional wisdom. The beauty of podcasting is that it allows you to express your unique voice and share your perspective with the world.

Building the Framework: Structuring Your Episodes

Once you have defined your podcast concept, it's time to move on to building the framework and structuring your episodes. The structure of your episodes is crucial in ensuring that your content flows smoothly and keeps your listeners engaged. So let's dive in and explore some key elements to consider when structuring your episodes.

First and foremost, you need to determine the length of your episodes. This will depend on various factors, including your podcast's topic, target audience, and format. Are you planning on sharing quick and digestible episodes that are 10-15 minutes long? Or do you prefer longer, in-depth discussions that range from 30 minutes to an hour? Understanding the ideal length for your episodes will help you maintain consistency and keep your audience's attention.

Next, consider the overall flow of your episodes. Begin with a captivating introduction that hooks your listeners and sets the tone for the episode. This could involve teasing the main topic or sharing an interesting anecdote to grab their attention from the start. Once you've hooked your audience, dive into the main content of your episode. This is where you deliver on the promise you made in your introduction.

To keep your episodes engaging, consider incorporating various segments or features. This could involve sharing personal stories, conducting interviews, answering listener questions, or discussing current events. By incorporating different elements into your episodes, you create a dynamic listening experience that keeps your audience entertained.

When structuring your episodes, it's also important to think about the order of your content. Consider how you can create a logical and coherent flow that takes your listeners on a journey. For example, if you're discussing a step-by-step process, make sure to present the information in a sequential order. This helps your audience follow along easily and makes it easier for them to take action based on your content.

Another crucial aspect of structuring your episodes is considering the inclusion of calls to action. What do you want your listeners to do after listening to your episode? Do you want them to visit your website, join your email list, or engage with you on social media? Including clear and compelling calls to action throughout your episode encourages your audience to take the desired action and further engage with your brand.

Lastly, don't forget about the importance of a strong conclusion. Wrap up your episode by summarizing the key points and leaving your listeners with a memorable takeaway. You can also tease upcoming episodes or share any additional resources that are relevant to the content you discussed.

When it comes to structuring your episodes, there is no one-size-fits-all approach. It's essential to experiment, iterate, and find a structure that works best for your podcast and your audience. Remember, the goal is to create a compelling and engaging listening experience that keeps your audience coming back for more. So take the time to plan and structure your episodes thoughtfully, and watch your podcast thrive.

The Power of a Name: How to Name Your Podcast

Naming your podcast may seem like a simple task, but don't underestimate the power of a name. Your podcast's name is the first impression your potential audience will have of your show, and it can make or break their decision to listen. So, how do you come up with a compelling and memorable name for your podcast? Let's explore some tips and strategies to help you choose the perfect name.

First, consider the theme and focus of your podcast. Your podcast's name should give your audience a clear indication of what your show is about. Think about the keywords or phrases that encapsulate the essence of your podcast's content. Is it a show about

28

entrepreneurship, personal development, or true crime? By incorporating relevant keywords or phrases into your podcast's name, you make it easier for potential listeners to find your show when they search for topics they're interested in.

Next, brainstorm a list of potential names that align with your podcast's concept. Don't be afraid to get creative and think outside the box. Look for unique angles or perspectives that you can incorporate into your name. A clever or intriguing name can pique curiosity and make people want to check out your show. Just make sure the name is still relevant to your podcast's content, so your audience doesn't feel misled.

Once you have a list of potential names, consider their length and ease of pronunciation. Shorter names tend to be more memorable and easier to share with others. Avoid using complex or hard-to-spell words that might confuse your audience. Keep it simple, catchy, and easy to remember.

Another strategy is to conduct market research and analyze your competitors' podcast names. Take a look at what other podcasts in your niche or industry are named and identify any naming trends. This will help you avoid using a name that's too similar to another podcast and enable you to differentiate your show. Aim for a name that stands out and captures your unique voice and perspective.

Additionally, consider the visual aspect of your

podcast's name. Your podcast's name will likely appear on various platforms, including podcast directories, social media, and your podcast's artwork. Make sure the name is visually appealing and can be easily recognized and remembered. Consider the use of fonts, colors, and imagery that complement your podcast's branding.

Lastly, don't be afraid to gather feedback from others. Share your list of potential names with friends, family, or even online communities and ask for their input. Sometimes an outside perspective can provide valuable insights and help you see things from a different angle.

Remember, choosing a name for your podcast is an important decision, but it doesn't have to be daunting. Take the time to brainstorm, research, and gather feedback until you find a name that feels right for your show. And once you've chosen a name, embrace it and let it become the cornerstone of your podcast's identity.

What Sets You Apart: Crafting a Unique Value Proposition

In the world of podcasting, standing out from the crowd is essential. With millions of podcasts available for listeners to choose from, you need to have a clear and compelling reason why people should tune into your show. This is where crafting a unique value proposition comes into play.

A value proposition is a concise statement that communicates the unique value your podcast offers to its audience. It answers the question, "What makes your show different from all the others?" Your value proposition should capture the essence of your podcast and entice potential listeners to give your show a chance.

To craft a unique value proposition, start by reflecting on what makes your podcast special. What do you bring to the table that no one else does? Maybe you have a unique perspective, extensive expertise, or a captivating storytelling style. Identify your strengths and think about how they can add value to your audience's listening experience.

Next, consider who your target audience is and what they're looking for in a podcast. What problems or challenges are they facing? How can your podcast provide solutions or insights that they won't find anywhere else? Understanding your audience's needs and desires will help you tailor your value proposition to resonate with them.

When crafting your value proposition, keep it simple and concise. Aim for a sentence or two that captures the essence of your podcast's unique offering. Use clear and persuasive language to communicate the benefits your audience will gain from listening to your show. Avoid vague or generic statements that could apply to any podcast. Instead, focus on what sets you apart and why listeners should choose your show over others.

One effective strategy is to use specific language and examples in your value proposition. Highlight the topics or themes your podcast covers and explain how you approach them differently. If you have a track record of success or notable achievements in your field, mention them to build credibility and show why you're an authority on the subject.

Another approach is to focus on the emotions and outcomes your podcast delivers. How will your show make your audience feel? Will it inspire, educate, entertain, or empower them? Communicate the benefits they can expect from listening to your episodes and how those benefits will enhance their lives.

Lastly, make sure your value proposition aligns with your podcast's overall branding and messaging. It should be consistent with the tone, style, and themes of your show. By presenting a cohesive and compelling value proposition, you create a strong and memorable impression that sets you apart from other podcasts in your niche.

Crafting a unique value proposition takes time and effort, but it's an essential step in planning a successful podcast. It helps you define your podcast's unique selling points and ensures that you're providing value to your audience. So take the time to reflect on what makes your show special, consider your audience's needs, and create a value proposition that sets you apart from the rest. With a compelling value proposition in place, you'll attract and engage listeners who resonate with your podcast's unique offering.

Putting it All Together: The Comprehensive Podcast Plan

Now that you have defined your podcast concept, structured your episodes, named your podcast, and crafted a unique value proposition, it's time to put it all together and create a comprehensive podcast plan. This plan will serve as a roadmap for your podcasting journey, ensuring that you stay organized and focused as you bring your show to life.

First, take a step back and look at the big picture. Think about your overarching goals for your podcast. What do you hope to achieve with your show? Are you looking to educate, entertain, inspire, or engage your audience? Understanding your goals will help you make strategic decisions throughout the planning and production process.

Next, create a timeline for your podcast. Determine how often you will release new episodes and establish a consistent schedule. This will help you build momentum and keep your audience engaged. Consider the time it takes to research, record, edit, and promote each episode, and allocate your resources accordingly.

Now it's time to dive into the nitty-gritty details. Break down your podcast plan into actionable steps. Consider the following elements:

1. Content Calendar: Map out your episode topics, guests, and any special segments or features you plan to include. This will help you stay organized and ensure that you have a steady stream of content ideas.

2. Production Workflow: Define the process for recording, editing, and publishing your episodes. Create a checklist of tasks to complete for each episode, and assign responsibilities to team members or yourself if you're a one-person show.

3. Promotion Strategy: Determine how you will promote your podcast to attract listeners. This could include social media marketing, guest appearances on other podcasts, collaborations with influencers or brands, or leveraging your existing network. Create a plan to consistently promote your show and build your audience.

4. Engagement Plan: Consider how you will engage with your listeners and build a community around your podcast. This could involve responding to comments and messages, hosting live Q&A sessions, or creating a Facebook group or Discord community. Find ways to make your audience feel connected and valued.

5. Monetization Strategy: If you're planning to monetize your podcast, outline your strategy. This could include sponsorships, affiliate marketing, merchandise sales, or launching a Patreon page. Research different monetization options and decide what aligns best with your podcast and audience.

6. Analytics and Evaluation: Set up a system to track and analyze the performance of your podcast. This could include monitoring download numbers, engagement metrics, and feedback from listeners. Use this data to identify areas for improvement and make informed decisions moving forward.

Remember, your podcast plan is a living document that can and should evolve over time. Be open to adapting your strategy based on feedback, trends in the industry, and the changing needs of your audience. Stay flexible and willing to experiment to find what works best for you and your show.

By putting together a comprehensive podcast plan, you set yourself up for success. You have a clear roadmap to guide you through the planning and production process, helping you stay organized and focused. So take the time to create your plan and start turning your podcasting dreams into reality.

4 Top Picks for Podcast Microphones and Editing Software

Podcasting has become a popular and effective way to share information, tell stories, and connect with audiences all over the world. And while the content of your podcast is crucial, the equipment and software you use can make or break the quality of your production. In this chapter, we will discuss the essential equipment and software needed for podcasting, with a focus on microphones and recording/editing software. Whether you're just starting out or looking to upgrade your current setup, we've got you covered with our top picks for podcasting equipment and software.

Picking the Perfect Podcast Microphone

When it comes to podcasting, the right microphone can make all the difference in the quality of your recordings. A high-quality microphone ensures that your voice comes through clearly and professionally, capturing all the nuances and subtleties that make your podcast unique. With so many options on the market, how do you choose the perfect podcast microphone for your needs? Here are some factors to consider:

1. Budget: Podcasting can be done on a wide range of budgets, and the price of microphones can vary significantly. Determine how much you are willing to invest in a microphone, keeping in mind that a higher

price tag often means better sound quality and durability. However, there are also budget-friendly options available that can still produce great results.

2. Microphone Type: There are two main types of microphones used in podcasting: dynamic and condenser. Dynamic microphones are rugged, durable, and great for recording in noisy environments. They are also more affordable than condenser microphones. On the other hand, condenser microphones are more sensitive and capture a wider frequency range, making them ideal for studio recording and capturing vocals with more detail and clarity.

3. Polar Pattern: The polar pattern refers to the microphone's sensitivity to sound from different directions. The most common polar patterns for podcasting are cardioid and omnidirectional. Cardioid microphones pick up sound primarily from the front, making them perfect for single-person or interview-style podcasts. Omnidirectional microphones capture sound from all directions, which is great for roundtable discussions or recording multiple speakers in the same room.

4. Connectivity: Consider how you will connect the microphone to your recording device. USB microphones are the easiest to use as they can be plugged directly into your computer or mobile device. XLR microphones, on the other hand, require an audio interface or mixer for connectivity, but they offer more

versatility and the ability to upgrade your setup in the future.

5. User-Friendly Features: Some microphones come with additional features such as built-in headphone jacks, gain control knobs, or mute buttons. These features can make your recording process more convenient and efficient, allowing you to monitor your sound in real-time and make adjustments as needed.

6. Reviews and Recommendations: Lastly, take the time to research and read reviews from other podcasters or audio professionals. They can provide valuable insights and recommendations based on their own experiences. Consider joining online podcasting communities or forums where you can ask for advice and gather feedback from fellow podcasters.

Ultimately, choosing the perfect podcast microphone comes down to your individual needs and preferences. It's important to find a microphone that suits your recording environment, style, and budget. By considering factors such as microphone type, polar pattern, connectivity, and user-friendly features, you can narrow down your options and find the microphone that will help you create high-quality, professional-sounding podcasts.

Recording and Editing Software: Making Your Podcast Shine

Once you have the perfect microphone for your

podcasting needs, it's time to focus on the recording and editing software that will take your podcast to the next level. The software you choose can greatly impact the quality, efficiency, and overall production value of your podcast. In this section, we will explore some of the best recording and editing software options available, so you can make your podcast shine.

One of the most popular and user-friendly recording and editing software for podcasters is Audacity. Audacity is a free, open-source program that offers a wide range of features and tools to enhance your podcast recordings. It allows you to record and edit audio with ease, and its intuitive interface makes it accessible to beginners and experienced podcasters alike. With Audacity, you can remove background noise, adjust volume levels, add effects, and export your final product in various formats. The best part? It's completely free.

If you're looking for a more professional and advanced recording and editing software, Adobe Audition is a top choice. Adobe Audition is a powerful digital audio workstation that provides a comprehensive set of tools and features for recording, editing, and mixing audio. With its intuitive interface and extensive functionality, Adobe Audition allows you to clean up your audio, apply effects, mix multiple tracks, and even perform advanced tasks like spectral editing and audio restoration. While Adobe Audition does come with a price tag, many podcasters consider it a worthwhile investment for its professional-grade capabilities.

For Mac users, GarageBand is an excellent option. GarageBand comes pre-installed on all Mac computers and offers a range of features specifically designed for podcasting. With GarageBand, you can easily record and edit your podcast episodes, add music and sound effects, and even create your own jingles and intros. GarageBand's user-friendly interface and robust editing tools make it a favorite among beginner podcasters.

If you're a Windows user, Reaper is a powerful and affordable digital audio workstation worth considering. Reaper offers a free 60-day trial and is known for its flexibility, efficiency, and low system requirements. It allows you to record and edit multiple tracks, apply effects, mix audio, and export your podcast episodes in various formats. Reaper also has an active online community that provides support and resources for podcasters of all levels.

No matter which recording and editing software you choose, it's important to familiarize yourself with its features and capabilities. Take the time to explore tutorials, watch videos, and experiment with different settings to make the most out of your software. Additionally, consider investing in a good pair of headphones to monitor your audio while editing. This will ensure that you catch any mistakes or inconsistencies and maintain a high level of quality in your final product.

Remember, the software you use is just as important as the microphone you choose. It can greatly impact the overall sound and production value of your podcast. So, take your time to research and test different options, and find the recording and editing software that best suits your needs and budget.

In the next section, we will discuss some essential additional equipment that can further enhance the sound quality of your podcast.

Tools of the Trade: Essential Additional Equipment for Quality Sound

When it comes to podcasting, having the right microphone and recording/editing software is essential. But there are a few additional tools that can further enhance the sound quality of your podcast and take your production to the next level. In this section, we will explore some essential additional equipment that every podcaster should consider.

1. Pop Filter: A pop filter is a must-have accessory for any podcast microphone. It helps reduce plosive sounds caused by hard consonant sounds like "p" and "b," which can cause distortion in your recordings. By placing a pop filter in front of your microphone, you can achieve a cleaner and more professional sound.

2. Shock Mount: A shock mount is a device that suspends your microphone, isolating it from any vibrations or movements that can create unwanted

noise in your recordings. It helps minimize handling noise and ensures that your microphone captures your voice accurately and without any disturbances. Using a shock mount can make a significant difference in the clarity and overall quality of your recordings.

3. Boom Arm: A boom arm is a versatile and adjustable microphone stand that allows you to position your microphone at the optimal height and distance from your mouth. It eliminates the need for a traditional desk stand and provides flexibility in terms of microphone placement. A boom arm helps reduce the risk of microphone bumps or accidental noise caused by movement during your podcast recording.

4. Acoustic Panels or Soundproofing: To achieve professional sound quality, it's crucial to minimize any echo or unwanted background noise in your recordings. Acoustic panels or soundproofing materials can help absorb and control sound reflections, ensuring a cleaner and more polished sound. Depending on your recording environment, you can opt for foam panels, diffusers, or even DIY solutions like blankets or pillows to improve the acoustics of your space.

5. Headphones: A good pair of closed-back headphones is an essential tool for podcasting. They allow you to monitor your audio in real-time, ensuring that your sound levels are balanced and there are no unwanted noises or technical issues. Invest in a

comfortable pair of headphones with accurate sound reproduction to catch any flaws or inconsistencies during your editing process.

6. External Audio Interface: If you're using an XLR microphone, an external audio interface is necessary for connecting your microphone to your computer. An audio interface converts analog signals from your microphone into digital data that your computer can process. It also provides features like preamp gain control, phantom power, and low-latency monitoring, which can significantly improve the quality and flexibility of your recordings.

Remember, while these additional tools can enhance your podcast's sound quality, they may not be necessary for every podcasting setup. Consider your specific needs, budget, and recording environment before investing in any additional equipment. It's always a good idea to start with the essentials and gradually upgrade your setup as you grow and gain experience in podcasting.

In the next section, we will discuss the importance of setting up an ideal recording space and share some tips and tricks to create a professional environment for your podcast recordings.

Setting up an Ideal Recording Space

Creating a professional recording space is essential for producing high-quality podcasts. While it's true that content is king, the environment in which you record can greatly impact the overall sound and professionalism of your episodes. In this section, we will discuss some tips and tricks to help you set up an ideal recording space for your podcast.

First and foremost, consider the location of your recording space. Ideally, you want to find a quiet room where you can minimize external noises such as traffic, construction, or household sounds. Choose a space that has good acoustics, meaning it's not too echoey or reverberant. A room with carpeting or curtains can help absorb sound and reduce reflections, resulting in cleaner and clearer recordings.

Once you have identified a suitable location, it's time to tackle the issue of background noise. Even the smallest noises can be picked up by your microphone and can be distracting to your listeners. To reduce unwanted noise, close any windows or doors to minimize outside sounds. If you can't eliminate all background noise, consider using a noise gate or noise reduction software during the editing process to help minimize its impact on your recordings.

Another important aspect to consider when setting up your recording space is the placement of your microphone. The distance and angle at which you position your microphone can greatly affect the sound quality. It's generally best to position your microphone at a distance of about 6 to 12 inches from your mouth.

This allows for optimal sound capture while minimizing the risk of plosive sounds or breath noise. Experiment with different microphone positions to find the one that suits your voice and recording style best.

Additionally, pay attention to the furniture and objects in your recording space. Hard surfaces such as desks, tables, or bookshelves can reflect sound and create unwanted echoes or reverberations. To combat this, consider adding soft furnishings like cushions, curtains, or foam panels to absorb sound and improve acoustics. If possible, invest in acoustic panels or soundproofing materials to further control sound reflections and create a more professional environment for your recordings.

Lighting is another factor to consider when setting up your recording space. While it may not directly impact the sound quality, good lighting can enhance the overall professionalism of your podcast. Natural light is always ideal, so try to position yourself near a window. If that's not possible, invest in soft, diffused lighting sources that illuminate your face without creating harsh shadows or glares.

Lastly, don't forget about comfort. Recording a podcast can take time, so make sure your recording space is comfortable and conducive to long recording sessions. Choose a chair that provides good back support and invest in a good microphone stand or boom arm that allows you to adjust the height and position of your microphone without straining your body. Creating a comfortable environment will not only make the recording process more enjoyable but also ensure consistent sound quality throughout your episodes.

Setting up an ideal recording space may require some experimentation and fine-tuning, but the results will be well worth the effort. By finding a quiet and acoustically treated space, optimizing your microphone placement, controlling background noise, and paying attention to lighting and comfort, you can create a professional recording environment that enhances the quality of your podcast.

Wrap-Up and Final Thoughts on Podcasting Equipment and Software

As we wrap up this blog post on essential podcasting equipment and software, it's clear that investing in the right tools can greatly enhance the quality of your podcast. From choosing the perfect microphone to finding the ideal recording and editing software, each decision you make contributes to creating a professional and engaging podcast.

When it comes to microphones, consider factors such as your budget, microphone type, polar pattern, and connectivity options. Finding the microphone that suits your needs and preferences will ensure that your voice comes through clearly and professionally, capturing all the nuances and subtleties that make your podcast unique.

For recording and editing software, there are plenty of options to choose from. Audacity, with its user-friendly interface and extensive features, is a popular choice for beginners and experienced podcasters alike. Adobe Audition offers advanced functionality for those looking for a more professional and sophisticated editing experience. GarageBand and Reaper are also excellent options for Mac and Windows users, respectively.

In addition to microphones and software, there are additional tools that can further enhance the sound quality of your podcast. A pop filter and shock mount can help reduce plosive sounds and handling noise, while a boom arm allows for optimal microphone placement. Acoustic panels or soundproofing materials can help control sound reflections and create a more polished sound. And of course, investing in a good pair of closed-back headphones and an external audio interface can greatly improve the quality and flexibility of your recordings.

Lastly, setting up an ideal recording space is crucial for producing high-quality podcasts. Finding a quiet room with good acoustics, minimizing background noise, optimizing microphone placement, and paying attention to lighting and comfort all contribute to creating a professional environment for your recordings.

Remember, the equipment and software you choose are important, but ultimately it's your content and storytelling that will captivate your audience. Use the tools and resources available to you to create a podcast that reflects your unique voice and resonates with your listeners.

Whether you're just starting out or looking to upgrade your current setup, we hope this blog post has provided valuable insights and recommendations for podcasting equipment and software. Remember to consider your individual needs, preferences, and budget when making decisions, and don't be afraid to experiment and learn as you go.

5 Mistakes Happen: How to Handle Imperfections in Your First Podcast

As you prepare to record your first episode, you may have a clear vision of the content you want to share with your audience. However, it's important to remember that mistakes and imperfections are bound to happen, especially when you're just starting out. But don't let that discourage you. In fact, learning how to handle these mistakes and imperfections can ultimately lead to a more successful and engaging podcast. In this chapter, we'll discuss some tips and strategies for handling imperfections in your first podcast recording, so you can confidently share your message with the world.

Planning Your First Podcast: Creating Content that Engages

This is your opportunity to showcase your unique voice and share your passion with the world. But where do you start?

The first step in planning your podcast is defining your niche or topic. What do you want to talk about? What are you passionate about? It's important to choose a subject that you're knowledgeable and enthusiastic about, as this will shine through in your episodes and resonate with your listeners. Take some time to brainstorm ideas and make a list of potential topics that align with your interests.

Once you have your niche or topic, it's time to dig deeper and identify your target audience. Who are you creating this podcast for? Who do you want to reach and connect with? Understanding your audience is crucial in developing content that will resonate with them. Think about their needs, interests, and pain points. What kind of information or entertainment can you provide that will be valuable to them? Tailor your content to address their needs and wants.

With your niche and target audience in mind, it's time to start planning your episode structure. A well-structured podcast will keep your listeners engaged and coming back for more. Start by outlining the main topics or segments you want to cover in each episode. This will help you stay organized and ensure a smooth flow throughout your episode. Consider adding an introduction at the beginning to set the stage and let your audience know what to expect. You can also include a conclusion at the end to summarize the main takeaways and wrap up the episode.

Now, let's talk about the format of your podcast. There are several different formats to choose from, including solo episodes, interviews, panel discussions, storytelling, and more. Each format has its own unique benefits and challenges, so it's important to choose one that aligns with your content and audience preferences. For example, if you're an expert in a particular field, conducting interviews with other experts can provide valuable insights for your audience. On the other hand, if you have a captivating personal story to share, a solo episode might be more appropriate. Experiment with different formats to see what works best for you and your audience.

In addition to the format, consider the length of your episodes. While there are no hard and fast rules, it's important to strike a balance between providing enough valuable content and not overwhelming your audience. Generally, podcasts range from 15 minutes to an hour, but feel free to adjust based on your topic and audience preferences. Remember, quality over quantity is key.

Finally, don't forget about the importance of branding and consistency. Choose a name, logo, and color scheme that reflects the tone and personality of your podcast. Consistency in your branding will help build recognition and establish your podcast as a trusted source of information or entertainment.

Embrace the Unexpected: Handling Mistakes during the Recording Session

Recording a podcast can be an exhilarating experience, but it's important to remember that mistakes and imperfections are bound to happen, especially when you're just starting out. While it's natural to feel a bit nervous about these mishaps, it's essential to embrace the unexpected and handle these mistakes with grace and confidence. In this section, we'll explore some strategies and tips for handling mistakes during your podcast recording session.

First and foremost, it's crucial to maintain a positive mindset. Mistakes are a part of the learning process, and every successful podcaster has encountered their fair share of blunders. Rather than beating yourself up over every slip-up, remind yourself that it's an opportunity to grow and improve. Embrace the unexpected and approach each mistake as a valuable learning experience.

One helpful strategy for handling mistakes during the recording session is to keep calm and carry on. When you make a mistake, resist the urge to immediately stop and start over. Instead, take a deep breath, gather your thoughts, and continue recording. Remember, your listeners are not expecting perfection. They want to connect with the real you, flaws and all. By gracefully moving past the mistake, you demonstrate authenticity and keep the flow of your podcast intact.

Another important aspect to consider when handling mistakes is the editing process. While some mistakes can be edited out, it's not necessary to eliminate every imperfection. In fact, leaving in some minor blunders can add character and make your podcast feel more relatable. As long as the overall message and content of your episode remain clear and engaging, a few mistakes here and there can be overlooked.

Additionally, it can be helpful to have a backup plan in case something goes wrong during your recording session. Technical issues such as audio glitches or interruptions can happen, so be prepared with contingency measures. Consider having spare equipment on hand or utilizing backup recording software to ensure you can continue your podcast without major disruptions. Having a backup plan not only alleviates stress but also shows your dedication to delivering quality content to your audience.

Incorporating humor is another effective way to handle mistakes during the recording session. If you stumble over your words or make a humorous slip-up, don't be afraid to laugh at yourself. Humor can help create a lighthearted atmosphere and make your podcast more enjoyable for both you and your listeners. Embracing these moments of imperfection can even become a signature part of your podcast's identity.

Finally, remember that mistakes are opportunities for growth and improvement. As you continue to record and produce episodes, you'll become more comfortable and confident in your abilities. Take note of the mistakes you make and use them as valuable feedback to refine your skills and processes. Each error is a stepping stone towards becoming a better podcaster and delivering high-quality content to your audience.

Tips for a Successful Recording Session: Best Practices to Follow

When it comes to recording your podcast, following some best practices can help ensure a smooth and successful recording session. Here are some tips to keep in mind:

1. Prepare and practice: Before hitting the record button, take some time to prepare and familiarize yourself with your content. Review your outline or script, make sure you have any necessary notes or resources nearby, and practice your delivery. This will help you feel more confident and prepared during the recording session.

2. Find a quiet and controlled environment: Background noise can be distracting and diminish the quality of your podcast. Choose a quiet location to record where you won't be interrupted by external noises such as traffic or loud neighbors. Consider using soundproofing materials or blankets to minimize echo and improve audio quality.

3. Invest in quality equipment: While you don't need to break the bank, investing in a good microphone and headphones can greatly improve the overall quality of your podcast. Look for microphones specifically designed for podcasting or broadcasting, as they often provide better sound reproduction. Headphones are important for monitoring audio levels and ensuring clear sound.

4. Use proper microphone technique: Position your microphone at the correct distance from your mouth to avoid distortions or muffled sounds. Aim for about six inches away from the microphone and speak directly into it. Avoid tapping or touching the microphone during the recording to prevent unwanted noise.

5. Warm up your voice: Just like any other performance, warming up your voice before recording can help you sound more clear and confident. Do some vocal exercises, practice speaking at different pitches and volumes, and stretch your facial muscles. This will help prevent strain and improve the quality of your voice during the recording.

6. Take breaks and stay hydrated: Recording a podcast can be physically and mentally demanding. Remember to take regular breaks to rest your voice, stretch, and relax. Stay hydrated by having water nearby to keep your vocal cords hydrated and prevent dryness or strain.

7. Monitor audio levels: Pay attention to your audio levels throughout the recording session. Keep an eye on the volume meters or use audio software to ensure that your levels are consistent and not too high or too low. This will help maintain a balanced and enjoyable listening experience for your audience.

8. Be mindful of your pacing: It's important to speak at a pace that is comfortable for both you and your listeners. Avoid rushing through your content or

speaking too slowly, as this can affect the engagement and comprehension of your audience. Take your time, pause when necessary, and vary your pacing to maintain interest.

9. Stay organized and focused: As you record your podcast, stay organized by referring to your outline or script. This will help you stay on track and cover all the topics or segments you planned. Avoid excessive ad-libbing or going off on tangents unless it adds value to your content.

10. Review and make adjustments: Once you've finished recording, take the time to review your episode and make any necessary adjustments. Listen for any technical issues, background noises, or moments that may need editing. Consider using editing software to enhance the overall quality of your podcast and remove any unnecessary or repetitive content.

By following these best practices, you can set yourself up for a successful recording session and create high-quality content for your audience. Remember, practice makes perfect, so don't be afraid to make adjustments and experiment until you find a recording routine that works best for you.

Improving Through Imperfections: Learning and Growing from your Mistakes

Mistakes are an inevitable part of any new endeavor, and starting a podcast is no exception. It's natural to feel frustrated or disappointed when you stumble over your words or make an error during your recording session. However, it's important to remember that mistakes can actually be valuable learning experiences that help you grow and improve as a podcaster. Instead of dwelling on your imperfections, embrace them and use them as stepping stones towards creating even better content for your audience.

One of the key ways to learn from your mistakes is to review and reflect on your recordings. Take the time to listen back to your episodes and pay attention to the areas where you stumbled or felt less confident. By actively listening to your recordings, you can identify patterns and areas for improvement. Maybe you notice that you tend to speak too quickly or stumble over certain phrases. Taking note of these tendencies allows you to consciously work on them in future recordings.

In addition to self-reflection, seeking feedback from others can be incredibly helpful in identifying areas for improvement. Reach out to trusted friends, family members, or fellow podcasters and ask them to listen to your episodes and provide constructive feedback. They may notice things that you overlooked or offer suggestions for how you can enhance your delivery or content. Remember, feedback is an opportunity for growth, so embrace it and use it to refine your skills.

It's also important to approach mistakes with a growth

mindset. Instead of viewing them as failures or signs of inadequacy, see them as opportunities to learn and develop. Every mistake is a chance to improve your podcasting abilities and provide better content for your audience. By reframing mistakes as learning opportunities, you can cultivate resilience and motivation to continue pushing forward.

Another way to learn from your mistakes is to take note of what works well in your episodes. Just as it's important to identify areas for improvement, it's equally important to recognize your strengths. Maybe you have a knack for storytelling or excel at asking thought-provoking interview questions. By recognizing and leveraging your strengths, you can enhance your podcasting skills and create content that truly resonates with your audience.

Lastly, remember that Rome wasn't built in a day. Becoming a successful podcaster takes time and practice. It's unrealistic to expect perfection right from the start. Embrace the fact that you are on a learning journey, and celebrate your progress along the way. With each recording session, you'll become more comfortable and confident, and your mistakes will become fewer and farther between.

In conclusion, imperfections and mistakes are a natural part of podcasting. Instead of viewing them as roadblocks, embrace them as opportunities for growth and improvement. Learn from your mistakes by actively listening to your recordings, seeking feedback from others, and approaching them with a growth mindset. Celebrate your strengths and acknowledge the progress you make along the way. By learning and growing from your mistakes, you can create a podcast that continually evolves and captivates your audience. Keep going, and remember that even the most successful podcasters started from humble beginnings.

6 Elevating Your Podcast to the Next Level

To truly stand out in the crowded world of podcasting, it's important to add those finishing touches that will elevate your podcast to the next level. In this chapter, we will discuss the essential editing and polishing techniques that will help take your podcast from good to great. From adding music and sound effects to creating a consistent brand sound, these tips will help make your podcast stand out and keep your listeners coming back for more.

Mastering the Basics: Effective Podcast Editing Techniques

So you've recorded your podcast and now it's time to dive into the editing process. This is where you can take your raw audio and turn it into a polished and professional episode that your listeners will love. Effective podcast editing techniques are crucial for creating a seamless and engaging listening experience. In this section, we'll explore some essential editing techniques that will help you master the basics of podcast editing.

First and foremost, it's important to ensure that your audio levels are balanced. Uneven audio levels can be distracting and make it difficult for listeners to fully engage with your content. Pay attention to the volume levels of your voice and any guests or co-hosts, as well as the levels of any background music or sound effects. Use a audio editing software to adjust the volume levels as needed, aiming for consistency throughout the episode.

Next, focus on removing any unwanted noises or distractions from your audio. This can include things like background noise, mouth clicks, ums and ahs, or any other audio imperfections that may detract from the quality of your podcast. Utilize your editing software's noise reduction tools to minimize these unwanted sounds and create a clean and polished final product.

Another important aspect of effective podcast editing is ensuring a smooth flow between different segments or sections of your episode. This can be achieved through the use of transitions. Transitions help to create a sense of cohesion and keep your listeners engaged from start to finish. Experiment with fade-ins, fade-outs, crossfades, or other transition effects to seamlessly move from one segment to another. Additionally, consider adding short music interludes or sound effects to further enhance the flow and transitions between different parts of your podcast.

Incorporating music into your podcast can also play a key role in enhancing the overall listening experience. Music can help set the tone, create emotional impact, and even act as a signature element of your podcast's brand. When choosing music for your podcast, consider the mood and style you want to convey. Find royalty-free music or work with a composer to create custom music that aligns with your podcast's theme and vibe. Integrate the music strategically throughout your episodes, using it as an introduction, background accompaniment, or as a way to mark transitions or important moments in your podcast.

Sound effects are another powerful tool to elevate your podcast. They can be used to emphasize certain moments, create atmosphere, or enhance storytelling. For example, adding the sound of a door opening and closing during a dramatic moment, or incorporating crowd cheers during an exciting announcement can make your podcast more immersive and engaging. Similar to music, make sure to use royalty-free sound effects or work with a sound designer to create custom sounds that align with your podcast's style and tone.

Finally, remember to give your podcast a final listen-through before publishing. This is an important step to catch any last-minute mistakes or inconsistencies that may have been missed during the editing process. Pay attention to the overall flow, audio quality, and the impact of your music and sound effects. By listening to your episode as a whole, you'll be able to make any final adjustments and ensure that your podcast is ready to be shared with the world.

Amplifying Engagement: Incorporating Music and Sound Effects

Now that you have mastered the basics of podcast editing, it's time to take your podcast to the next level by incorporating music and sound effects. Music and sound effects are powerful tools that can amplify engagement and enhance the overall listening experience for your audience. In this section, we will explore the different ways you can use music and sound effects to captivate your listeners and create a more immersive podcast.

Music is a fundamental component of any podcast. It sets the tone, creates emotional impact, and can even act as a signature element of your podcast's brand. When choosing music for your podcast, consider the mood and style you want to convey. Whether you're going for a suspenseful thriller or a light-hearted comedy, finding the right music can greatly enhance the overall atmosphere of your podcast. There are plenty of websites that offer royalty-free music for podcasts, or you can work with a composer to create custom music that aligns perfectly with your podcast's theme and vibe.

Integrating music strategically throughout your episodes can make a world of difference. Consider using music as an introduction to set the stage for your listeners. A catchy and memorable intro can help to immediately grab their attention and pique their interest. You can also use music as background accompaniment during certain segments or as a way to mark transitions between different parts of your podcast. By using music strategically, you can create a more dynamic and engaging listening experience for your audience.

In addition to music, sound effects can add depth and texture to your podcast. Sound effects can be used to emphasize certain moments, create atmosphere, or enhance storytelling. For example, adding the sound of rain during a reflective monologue or incorporating the sound of footsteps in a suspenseful scene can transport your listeners into the world you are creating. Just like with music, it's important to use royalty-free sound effects or work with a sound designer to create custom sounds that align with your podcast's style and tone.

When using sound effects, it's important to strike a balance. Too many sound effects can be overwhelming and distract from the content of your podcast. On the other hand, too few sound effects can make your podcast feel flat and monotonous. Experiment with different sound effects to find the right balance for your podcast. Whether it's a door creaking, a phone ringing, or a crowd cheering, the right sound effects can enhance the storytelling and create a more immersive experience for your listeners.

Remember, the goal is to engage your audience and keep them coming back for more. When incorporating music and sound effects, be mindful of the impact they have on the overall listening experience. They should enhance your podcast, not overpower it. Aim for a seamless integration that complements your content and adds value to the listener.

Crafting Your Identity: Establishing a Consistent Brand Sound

In the vast world of podcasting, it's not just about creating great content, but also about creating a brand identity that sets you apart from the rest. Your podcast should have a unique sound that becomes synonymous with your brand. It's important to establish a consistent brand sound that resonates with your listeners and helps to build a loyal following. In this section, we will explore how you can craft your identity by establishing a consistent brand sound for your podcast.

One of the first steps in establishing a consistent brand sound is choosing the right music that aligns with your podcast's theme and vibe. Music has the power to evoke emotions and set the tone for your podcast. Whether you're going for a relaxed and introspective feel or a high-energy and upbeat atmosphere, the music you choose should reflect the essence of your podcast. Consider the genre, tempo, and overall style of the music that will resonate with your target audience. It's important to find the right balance between being on-trend and staying true to your podcast's unique identity.

Once you've chosen the right music, it's crucial to use it strategically throughout your episodes. Your podcast should have a signature sound or theme music that is instantly recognizable to your listeners. This could be a short musical intro or outro that plays at the beginning or end of each episode, or it could be a recurring musical interlude that marks different segments of your podcast. By consistently incorporating your chosen music into your episodes, you establish a cohesive and recognizable brand sound that becomes synonymous with your podcast.

In addition to music, consider incorporating sound effects that align with your podcast's brand. Sound effects can add depth and texture to your episodes, creating a more immersive listening experience for your audience. Whether it's the sound of waves crashing for a podcast about surfing or the sound of a crowd cheering for a podcast about sports, the right sound effects can help reinforce your brand identity and create a unique atmosphere for your listeners. Be sure to choose sound effects that enhance your content and add value to the overall listening experience, rather than using them just for the sake of it.

Consistency is key when it comes to establishing a brand sound. Your podcast should have a consistent tone and style throughout all of your episodes. This includes the way you speak, the pacing of your episodes, and the overall atmosphere that you create.

By consistently delivering high-quality content that aligns with your podcast's brand, you build trust and credibility with your audience. They know what to expect when they tune in to your podcast, and this helps to create a loyal following of listeners who come back for more.

Another aspect to consider when establishing a consistent brand sound is the overall production quality of your podcast. This includes the clarity of your audio, the use of professional editing techniques, and the overall polish of your episodes. A well-produced podcast conveys professionalism and attention to detail, which in turn enhances your brand image. It's important to invest in quality equipment, such as microphones and audio editing software, to ensure that your podcast sounds professional and polished. This attention to production quality not only adds to the overall listening experience but also helps to solidify your brand identity.

Lastly, engage with your audience to reinforce your brand identity. Interact with your listeners on social media platforms, respond to comments and messages, and ask for feedback. By actively engaging with your audience, you create a sense of community and strengthen the connection between your brand and your listeners. Encourage them to share their thoughts, suggestions, and experiences related to your podcast. This not only helps to establish your brand identity but also allows you to fine-tune your content and improve your podcast based on your listeners' feedback.

In conclusion, crafting your identity through establishing a consistent brand sound is crucial in the world of podcasting. Your podcast should have a unique sound that reflects your brand and resonates with your audience. Choose music and sound effects that align with your podcast's theme and style, and use them strategically to create a cohesive and recognizable brand sound. Be consistent in your tone, style, and overall production quality to build trust and loyalty with your audience. Finally, engage with your listeners to strengthen the connection between your brand and your audience.

7 Grab Attention with Eye-Catching Podcast Artwork and Description

As the podcast industry continues to grow and become more saturated, it's becoming increasingly important for podcasters to stand out and grab the attention of potential listeners. One of the most effective ways to do this is through eye-catching artwork and a compelling podcast description. Your podcast's artwork and description are often the first things that people will see when deciding whether or not to give your show a chance, so it's crucial to make a strong first impression. In this chapter, we'll discuss the key elements of creating eye-catching artwork, crafting an engaging description, and how to effectively brand your podcast across various platforms.

The Importance of Attractive Podcast Artwork

In today's podcast landscape, where new shows are being launched every day, it's crucial for podcasters to find ways to stand out from the crowd and catch the attention of potential listeners. While the quality of your content is undoubtedly important, it's equally essential to make a strong first impression through eye-catching artwork.

Your podcast artwork is like the cover of a book - it's the first thing people see and judge your show by. It's your opportunity to convey the essence of your podcast and attract listeners with just one glance. The importance of attractive podcast artwork cannot be overstated. It serves as a visual representation of your brand and sets the tone for what listeners can expect.

Imagine scrolling through a podcast directory or app. Hundreds, if not thousands, of thumbnails and covers fill the screen, all vying for your attention. In this sea of options, how does a podcast catch your eye? It's all about visual appeal and making an instant connection.

The key to creating attractive podcast artwork is finding a balance between eye-catching design and communicating your podcast's content. The design should reflect the genre, mood, and personality of your show. Use colors, fonts, and images that are relevant and resonate with your target audience. For example, if you host a true crime podcast, you might choose dark and moody colors with mysterious imagery. On the other hand, if you have a comedy podcast, bright and bold colors with playful illustrations could be more suitable.

Additionally, simplicity and clarity are crucial in podcast artwork. Avoid cluttered designs that confuse or overwhelm potential listeners. Opt for a clean and focused layout that communicates the essence of your podcast at a glance. Remember, your artwork should be easily recognizable, even at a small size.

Another aspect to consider when designing your podcast artwork is the use of typography. The font you choose should align with the overall aesthetic of your show while remaining legible and easy to read. Bold and unique typography can make your podcast stand out from the crowd, but ensure it doesn't sacrifice readability.

When creating your podcast artwork, it's essential to keep in mind that it will appear in various contexts. It will be displayed on podcast platforms, social media, websites, and potentially even merchandise. As a result, it should be versatile enough to work well across different mediums. Test your artwork in different sizes and formats to ensure it looks great in every situation.

Crafting a Compelling Podcast Description

Once you've grabbed someone's attention with your eye-catching podcast artwork, the next step is to keep them engaged with a compelling podcast description. Your podcast description is like the blurb on the back of a book - it should entice potential listeners to click that play button and give your show a chance.

When crafting your podcast description, it's essential to be concise yet informative. You only have a few sentences to hook your audience and make them curious about what your show has to offer. Start by clearly stating the topic or theme of your podcast. This helps potential listeners quickly understand what your show is about and whether it aligns with their interests.

Next, highlight the unique value or perspective that

your podcast brings to the table. What sets your show apart from others in the same genre? Is it your expert guests, your storytelling style, or your comedic approach? This is your opportunity to showcase what makes your podcast special and why listeners should choose to spend their time with you.

It's also important to consider your target audience when crafting your podcast description. Who are you trying to reach? What are their interests, pain points, or passions? Speak directly to them in your description and address the specific benefits they will gain from listening to your show. Make them feel like your podcast was created just for them.

In addition to capturing your podcast's essence, don't forget to include a call to action in your description. This could be as simple as encouraging listeners to subscribe, rate, and review your podcast. It could also be directing them to your website for additional resources or inviting them to engage with you on social media. By including a call to action, you're inviting listeners to take the next step in their journey with your podcast.

Lastly, always make sure to proofread and edit your podcast description. Typos and grammatical errors can make your show appear unprofessional and can turn potential listeners away. Take the time to ensure that your description is well-written, clear, and free of errors. You want to make a positive first impression and show that you care about the quality of your content.

Remember, your podcast description is your chance to make a connection with potential listeners. It should be engaging, informative, and enticing. Take the time to craft a compelling description that accurately represents your podcast and makes people eager to hit that play button.

In the next section, we'll explore the power of effective podcast branding and how it can help you stand out in the crowded podcasting landscape.

The Power of Effective Podcast Branding

In the increasingly competitive podcasting landscape, effective branding is the key to standing out from the crowd and making a lasting impression on your audience. Podcast branding goes beyond just having a catchy name or a visually appealing logo. It's about creating a consistent and memorable identity that reflects the essence of your podcast and resonates with your target audience.

Effective podcast branding helps you build trust and loyalty with your listeners. When your branding is cohesive and recognizable across different platforms, it establishes a sense of familiarity and professionalism. This not only makes your podcast more memorable but also positions you as a reliable source of valuable content.

One of the first steps in effective podcast branding is defining your podcast's unique selling proposition (USP). What sets your show apart from others in the same genre? Is it your storytelling style, your expertise, or the way you engage with your audience? Identifying your USP allows you to develop a branding strategy that highlights your podcast's strengths and communicates its value to potential listeners.

Once you've defined your USP, it's important to align your podcast's visual elements with your brand identity. This includes your podcast artwork, logo, color palette, and typography. Consistency in these visual elements creates a cohesive and recognizable brand image. Your podcast artwork, in particular, should reflect the tone and genre of your show while capturing the attention of potential listeners.

In addition to visual branding, consider the use of sonic branding. This involves creating a unique audio signature that becomes synonymous with your podcast. It could be a catchy intro jingle, a distinctive sound effect, or a memorable catchphrase. Sonic branding helps reinforce your podcast's identity and creates a sense of familiarity for your listeners.

Another important aspect of effective podcast branding is consistency across different platforms. Your podcast should have a cohesive presence on podcast directories, social media platforms, and your own website. Use the same branding elements, such as your logo and color palette, across these platforms to create a unified and recognizable identity. Consistency in branding not only makes it easier for your audience to find and recognize your podcast but also strengthens your overall brand image.

Lastly, don't forget to engage with your audience and build a community around your podcast. Encourage listeners to interact with you through social media, email, or live events. Actively participating in conversations related to your podcast's topic can further establish your authority and credibility. Building a loyal community around your podcast strengthens your brand and helps spread the word about your show.

Guidelines for Cross-platform Podcast Branding

Once you have created eye-catching artwork and crafted a compelling podcast description, it's time to focus on cross-platform branding to ensure consistency and recognition across different platforms. Cross-platform podcast branding is crucial for building a cohesive and memorable identity for your show.

First and foremost, it's important to use the same branding elements, such as your podcast artwork, logo, color palette, and typography, across all platforms. Consistency in visual elements creates a unified and recognizable brand image. When potential listeners see your podcast artwork or logo, they should immediately associate it with your show. This helps establish a sense of familiarity and professionalism, making your podcast more memorable.

When implementing your branding across different platforms, pay close attention to the specific requirements and guidelines of each platform. For example, podcast directories may have specific image dimensions or file size limitations for your artwork. Social media platforms may have their own formatting guidelines for profile pictures and cover photos. Make sure to adapt your branding elements accordingly to ensure a consistent and visually appealing presence.

Another important aspect of cross-platform branding is to optimize your podcast's SEO (search engine optimization) across different platforms. Use relevant keywords in your podcast title, description, and episode titles to improve your visibility in search results. Additionally, consider creating a unique and catchy podcast URL that aligns with your branding and is easy for listeners to remember.

In addition to visual branding, consider incorporating sonic branding into your podcast. Create a distinctive intro jingle, sound effect, or catchphrase that becomes synonymous with your show. Sonic branding helps reinforce your podcast's identity and creates a sense of familiarity for your listeners. Use these audio elements consistently across your episodes, social media content, and any promotional materials.

Engaging with your audience is a crucial aspect of

cross-platform podcast branding. Actively participate in conversations related to your podcast's topic on social media platforms, online communities, and forums. Respond to comments, questions, and feedback from your listeners to establish a connection and build a loyal community around your show. Encourage listeners to interact with you through social media, email, or even live events. By engaging with your audience, you strengthen your brand and foster a sense of community around your podcast.

Lastly, regularly evaluate and adapt your cross-platform branding strategy. Keep track of how your branding elements perform on different platforms and make adjustments as needed. Stay updated on the latest design trends and platform guidelines to ensure that your branding remains fresh and relevant. By continually refining and optimizing your cross-platform branding, you can strengthen your podcast's identity and stand out in the crowded podcasting landscape.

Success Stories: Examples of Eye-Catching Podcast Art and Branding

Podcast artwork and branding play a crucial role in capturing the attention of potential listeners and establishing a strong and memorable presence in the podcasting landscape. In this section, we will explore some success stories of podcasts that have effectively utilized eye-catching artwork and branding to stand out from the crowd.

One podcast that excels in eye-catching artwork is "Crime Scene Chronicles". The artwork features a dark and mysterious color palette, with a close-up image of a fingerprint covered in blood. The combination of the eerie imagery and the bold typography instantly captures the essence of the true crime genre and entices potential listeners to explore the podcast further. This artwork effectively communicates the tone and mood of the show, making it an excellent example of attractive podcast artwork.

Another success story in podcast artwork and branding is "The Funny Hour Podcast". This comedy podcast stands out with its bright and playful artwork. The artwork features colorful illustrations of comedic symbols and a bold, quirky typography. The use of vibrant colors and fun illustrations perfectly captures the lighthearted and entertaining nature of the show. It immediately grabs the attention of potential listeners and gives a clear indication of the show's genre.

When it comes to crafting a compelling podcast description, "The Mindset Masterclass" is a standout example. The description begins with a clear statement of the podcast's topic, which is personal development and self-improvement. It then highlights the unique value of the show, emphasizing its expert guests and actionable strategies for achieving success. The description is written in a conversational tone, addressing the target audience directly and making them feel like the podcast was created just for them. It also includes a strong call to action, encouraging listeners to subscribe and engage with the show further. Overall, "The Mindset Masterclass" demonstrates the power of a concise yet informative podcast description that entices potential listeners to hit that play button.

One podcast that exemplifies effective podcast branding is "The Healthy Living Hour". This podcast utilizes a consistent visual identity across all platforms, with a clean and modern logo, a cohesive color palette, and a professional typography choice. The visual elements align perfectly with the show's focus on health and wellness. The podcast also incorporates sonic branding by using a catchy and memorable intro jingle that is consistently used in every episode. This sonic branding element helps establish a strong brand identity and creates a sense of familiarity for listeners.

Overall, these success stories demonstrate the power of eye-catching artwork, compelling podcast descriptions, and effective branding in capturing the attention of potential listeners and establishing a strong presence in the podcasting landscape. By investing time and effort into these key elements, podcasters can differentiate themselves from the competition, attract a loyal audience, and create a lasting impression in the minds of their listeners.

8 The Ultimate Guide to Podcast Hosting: Comparing Your Options

In the ever-growing world of podcasting, it is essential to have a reliable and user-friendly hosting platform to share your audio content with the world. With numerous hosting options available, it can be overwhelming to choose the right one for your podcast. In this guide, we will compare the top podcast hosting platforms, discuss how to upload, and manage your episodes, and understand the importance of RSS feeds in reaching your audience. Whether you are a seasoned podcaster or just starting, this guide will help you make an informed decision and take your podcast to the next level.

Navigating Your Choices: An Overview of Podcast Hosting Platforms

As a podcaster, choosing the right hosting platform is crucial for the success of your show. With so many options available, it can be overwhelming to navigate through the choices. In this section, we will provide you with an overview of the top podcast hosting platforms, helping you make an informed decision and find the perfect fit for your needs.

One of the most popular podcast hosting platforms is Podbean. Known for its user-friendly interface and comprehensive features, Podbean is a favorite among podcasters of all levels. It offers unlimited storage, customizable websites, and easy integration with popular podcast directories. Additionally, Podbean provides detailed analytics and monetization options, allowing you to track your podcast's performance and even make money from your content.

Another top hosting platform is Libsyn. Known for its reliability and extensive distribution network, Libsyn has been a go-to choice for many podcasters. It offers various pricing plans to accommodate different needs, along with robust analytics and audience engagement tools. Libsyn also provides seamless integration with social media platforms, making it easier to promote your podcast and connect with your audience.

If you're looking for a platform that offers a combination of simplicity and advanced features, Anchor might be the right choice for you. Anchor is known for its intuitive interface, making it easy to record, edit, and publish episodes directly from your phone. It also provides free hosting and distribution to major podcast platforms, as well as monetization options through sponsorships and listener support.

For podcasters who value flexibility and control over their hosting, Blubrry is a top choice. Blubrry offers advanced podcasting features, such as customizable RSS feeds and comprehensive statistics. It also allows for seamless integration with WordPress websites, making it a popular choice among podcasters who want to maintain full ownership of their content.

Finally, if you're a podcaster who prioritizes simplicity and affordability, Buzzsprout may be the hosting platform for you. Buzzsprout offers a user-friendly interface, along with a step-by-step guide on uploading and managing your episodes. It also provides free hosting for 90 days, allowing you to test out the platform before committing to a paid plan.

In this section, we've covered just a few of the many podcast hosting platforms available. Each platform offers its own unique set of features and benefits, so it's important to consider your specific needs and goals when making a decision. Now that you have an overview of the top hosting platforms, you can move on to the next section, where we will dive deeper into the key features and comparisons of each platform.

A Closer Look at Popular Hosting Options: Key Features and Comparisons

When it comes to podcast hosting platforms, there are a multitude of options available to suit every podcaster's needs. In this section, we will take a closer look at some of the most popular hosting options, exploring their key features and making comparisons to help you make an informed decision.

Let's start with Podbean, a widely used platform known for its user-friendly interface and comprehensive features. With Podbean, you get unlimited storage for your audio files, which means you can upload as many episodes as you want without worrying about running out of space. Additionally, Podbean offers customizable websites, allowing you to create a unique online presence for your podcast. The platform also seamlessly integrates with popular podcast directories, making it easy for your audience to find and subscribe to your show. Detailed analytics are another highlight of Podbean, giving you insights into your podcast's performance and helping you make informed decisions for growth. Not to mention, Podbean also offers monetization options, enabling you to make money from your content through advertising and premium subscriptions.

Next up is Libsyn, a hosting platform renowned for its reliability and extensive distribution network. With Libsyn, you can trust that your episodes will be delivered seamlessly to various podcast directories, ensuring maximum reach and exposure. The platform offers different pricing plans to suit your needs, making it accessible for podcasters of all levels. Another key feature of Libsyn is its robust analytics, allowing you to track your podcast's performance in terms of downloads, engagement, and geographical reach. Libsyn also provides tools for audience engagement, including the ability to offer bonus content and collect listener feedback. Additionally, Libsyn seamlessly integrates with social media platforms, making it easier for you to promote your podcast and connect with your audience.

If simplicity and convenience are your priorities, Anchor is a hosting platform that stands out. Anchor's intuitive interface allows you to record, edit, and publish your episodes directly from your phone, eliminating the need for complex editing software. The platform also offers free hosting and distribution to major podcast platforms, saving you the hassle of manually submitting your show to multiple directories. Anchor provides monetization options as well, such as sponsorships and listener support, giving you the opportunity to generate revenue from your podcast. With its user-friendly approach and various features, Anchor is a popular choice for both beginners and seasoned podcasters.

For podcasters who value flexibility and control, Blubrry is a top hosting choice. Blubrry offers advanced podcasting features, including customizable RSS feeds and comprehensive statistics. This allows you to tailor your podcast's distribution and analytics according to your specific needs. Additionally, Blubrry seamlessly integrates with WordPress websites, making it a popular choice for podcasters who want to maintain full ownership of their content. Blubrry also provides media hosting with unlimited storage, ensuring that you never have to compromise on the quality or quantity of your episodes.

Lastly, if simplicity and affordability are your top considerations, Buzzsprout is worth considering. Buzzsprout offers a user-friendly interface, along with a step-by-step guide on uploading and managing your episodes. The platform provides free hosting for the first 90 days, giving you a chance to test it out before committing to a paid plan.

Step-by-step Guide on Uploading and Managing Episodes on Your Chosen Platform

Once you have chosen the perfect podcast hosting platform for your show, it's time to dive into the exciting process of uploading and managing your episodes. In this step-by-step guide, we will walk you through the process, ensuring that you have all the tools and knowledge to navigate your chosen platform with ease.

Step 1: Sign up and create an account

The first step is to sign up and create an account on your chosen podcast hosting platform. This usually involves providing your email address, choosing a username and password, and agreeing to the platform's terms and conditions. Once you have completed the sign-up process, you will have access to your hosting dashboard.

Step 2: Prepare your audio files

Before you can upload your episodes, it's essential to have your audio files ready. Make sure your episodes are saved in a compatible format, such as MP3 or WAV. You may also want to consider editing your episodes beforehand to ensure the best possible sound quality.

Step 3: Upload your episodes

Now that your audio files are ready, it's time to upload them to your hosting platform. In your hosting dashboard, you will typically find an option to upload new episodes. Click on this option and select the audio files you wish to upload. Depending on the size of your files and your internet connection, the uploading process may take a few minutes.

Step 4: Add episode details

Once your episodes are uploaded, you will need to provide some essential details for each episode. This typically includes the episode title, description, and any relevant tags or keywords. You may also have the option to add episode artwork, which can help make your episodes more visually appealing.

Step 5: Customize your podcast page

Many hosting platforms allow you to customize your podcast's page, giving it a unique and personalized look. Take some time to explore the customization options provided by your chosen platform, such as choosing a theme, adding a logo, or changing the layout. This will help make your podcast page more visually appealing and reflect the branding of your show.

Step 6: Submit your podcast to directories

To reach a wider audience, it's essential to submit your podcast to popular podcast directories such as Apple Podcasts, Spotify, and Google Podcasts. Most hosting platforms offer easy integration with these directories, allowing you to submit your show with just a few clicks. Simply follow the instructions provided by your hosting platform to submit your podcast to the directories of your choice.

Step 7: Monitor and manage your episodes

Once your episodes are live, it's crucial to monitor and manage them regularly. This includes keeping track of your download and engagement statistics, responding to listener feedback, and making any necessary edits or updates to your episodes. Your hosting platform should provide you with detailed analytics and tools to help you manage your episodes effectively.

By following this step-by-step guide, you will be well-equipped to upload and manage your episodes on your chosen podcast hosting platform. Remember to take advantage of the platform's features and tools to optimize your podcast's performance and reach. With a user-friendly hosting platform and your newfound knowledge, you are ready to take your podcast to the next level.

RSS Feeds Demystified: Understanding Its Importance in Podcast Hosting

In the world of podcasting, you may have heard the

term "RSS feeds" thrown around. But what exactly are RSS feeds, and why are they so important in the realm of podcast hosting? In this section, we will demystify RSS feeds and explain their significance in helping you reach your audience.

To put it simply, RSS (Really Simple Syndication) feeds are a technology that allows your podcast episodes to be distributed and subscribed to by your audience. Think of it as a digital delivery system that ensures your content reaches your listeners' devices in a timely and convenient manner.

One of the key benefits of RSS feeds is that they enable automatic updates. When you upload a new episode to your podcast hosting platform, the RSS feed is automatically updated, notifying all subscribed devices that a new episode is available. This eliminates the need for your audience to manually check for new episodes and ensures that they never miss a beat.

But the importance of RSS feeds goes beyond mere convenience. They also play a vital role in expanding your podcast's reach. When you submit your podcast to popular directories such as Apple Podcasts, Spotify, and Google Podcasts, these directories rely on RSS feeds to access and display your episodes to their users. Without a properly functioning RSS feed, your podcast may not be listed in these directories, limiting your potential audience.

In addition to distribution, RSS feeds also provide

important metadata about your episodes. This metadata includes information such as the episode title, description, duration, and release date. Podcast directories and apps use this information to categorize and organize podcasts, making it easier for users to discover and subscribe to new shows. Therefore, ensuring that your RSS feed is accurately and comprehensively filled out is crucial for optimizing your podcast's discoverability.

Another significant aspect of RSS feeds is their role in tracking analytics. Most podcast hosting platforms provide detailed analytics on how your episodes are performing, such as the number of downloads, listener engagement, and geographical reach. These analytics are powered by your RSS feed, which provides data on how many times your episodes have been accessed and by whom. By analyzing these statistics, you can gain valuable insights into your audience's preferences and tailor your content accordingly.

It's important to note that your chosen podcast hosting platform is responsible for generating and maintaining your RSS feed. Therefore, when selecting a hosting platform, it's crucial to ensure that they offer reliable RSS feed capabilities. Look for platforms that provide customizable RSS feeds, as this allows you to optimize your feed's appearance and metadata. Additionally, make sure that your chosen platform offers seamless integration with popular podcast directories, ensuring that your RSS feed is effectively distributed.

How to Choose the Right Podcast Hosting Platform for Your Needs

When it comes to choosing the right podcast hosting platform for your needs, there are several factors to consider. While we have provided an overview of some of the top hosting platforms, the final decision ultimately depends on your specific requirements and goals. In this section, we will discuss the key considerations to keep in mind when selecting a podcast hosting platform.

First and foremost, think about your budget. While some hosting platforms offer free options, they often come with limitations on storage, bandwidth, or features. If you are just starting and want to test the waters, a free plan might be suitable. However, if you are serious about podcasting and plan to produce and upload a large number of episodes, it may be worth investing in a paid plan that offers unlimited storage and advanced features.

Next, consider the features and tools offered by each hosting platform. Think about what is most important to you and your podcast. Do you need customizable websites, detailed analytics, or monetization options? Are you looking for integration with popular podcast directories or social media platforms? Take the time to explore each platform's offerings and assess how well they align with your podcasting needs.

Another crucial factor to consider is ease of use. As a

podcaster, you want a hosting platform that is intuitive and user-friendly, especially if you are just starting. Look for platforms that offer a simple and straightforward interface, easy episode uploading and management, and clear instructions or tutorials. Some platforms even offer mobile apps, allowing you to record, edit, and publish episodes directly from your phone.

Additionally, consider the scalability and flexibility of the hosting platform. As your podcast grows and evolves, you may need more storage, advanced features, or integration options. Look for platforms that can accommodate your future needs and allow for easy upgrades or customization.

Furthermore, take into account the platform's reputation and reliability. Research user reviews and feedback to get an idea of other podcasters' experiences with the hosting platform. Look for platforms that have a track record of uptime and reliable customer support.

Lastly, consider the platform's customer support and resources. Look for platforms that offer responsive customer support, whether through email, chat, or phone. Additionally, check if the platform provides resources such as tutorials, documentation, or a knowledge base to help you navigate any challenges or questions you may have.

By considering these factors, you can narrow down

your options and make an informed decision when choosing the right podcast hosting platform for your needs. Remember, the perfect platform for someone else may not be the best fit for you, so take the time to evaluate your requirements and prioritize what matters most to you. With the right hosting platform, you can confidently upload, manage, and share your podcast episodes, reaching your audience and taking your podcast to the next level.

9 How to Build Anticipation for Your Podcast Launch

Before you hit that publish button, there's an important step that can make or break the success of your podcast: building anticipation. Just like a movie or book release, creating buzz and excitement around your podcast launch can help attract a larger audience and set the tone for your show. In this chapter, we'll discuss how to unleash the buzz and build anticipation for your podcast launch. From creating teaser content to crafting an engaging launch episode, we've got you covered on all the essential strategies to make your podcast debut a hit.

The Power of Teasers: Building Excitement for Your Podcast Launch

Creating anticipation and excitement for your podcast launch is crucial to attract a larger audience and generate buzz around your show. One powerful tool in your podcast promotion arsenal is the use of teasers. These bite-sized pieces of content can captivate your potential listeners and leave them eagerly anticipating the release of your first episode.

So, what exactly is a teaser and how can it help you build excitement for your podcast launch? A teaser is a short preview or sneak peek of what your podcast is all about. It's designed to pique the interest of your target audience and give them a taste of what's to come. Just like movie trailers or book excerpts, teasers create anticipation and build hype.

To effectively utilize teasers, you need to focus on creating compelling content that showcases the unique value proposition of your podcast. Here are some strategies to consider:

1. Share snippets of your best moments: Select some of the most engaging and captivating moments from your upcoming episodes and turn them into teasers. These snippets should showcase the essence of your podcast and leave your potential listeners wanting more. Make sure to include a strong call-to-action at the end of each teaser, inviting them to subscribe or follow your podcast.

2. Highlight your guests: If your podcast features interviews or conversations with guests, leverage their names and expertise to build anticipation. Create teasers that introduce your guests, their background, and what they will bring to the conversation. This can create excitement among their fans and followers, who will be curious to hear their perspectives in your upcoming episodes.

3. Use audio production techniques: Utilize audio production techniques like sound effects, music, or narration to enhance the impact of your teasers. These techniques can help create a dynamic and immersive experience for your potential listeners, leaving them

intrigued and excited to tune in to your podcast.

4. Offer exclusive content: To reward your early supporters and build anticipation, consider offering exclusive teaser content that is only available to those who subscribe or sign up before your official launch. This can be bonus episodes, behind-the-scenes footage, or exclusive interviews. By offering something special, you create a sense of exclusivity and value that can drive more interest and anticipation for your podcast.

5. Leverage social media: Social media platforms are excellent tools for promoting your teasers and building anticipation for your podcast launch. Share your teasers on platforms like Instagram, TikTok, X, Facebook, and LinkedIn, and encourage your followers to share them with their networks. You can also create short teaser videos or graphics to make your teasers visually appealing and shareable.

Remember, the goal of your teasers is to create a buzz around your podcast and generate excitement among your target audience. Be strategic in how you release your teasers, spacing them out leading up to your launch date to keep the anticipation building. Engage with your potential listeners, answer their questions, and create a sense of community around your upcoming podcast.

In the next section, we'll dive into the process of crafting a captivating launch episode that will hook your listeners from the very beginning.

From Idea to Airwaves: Crafting a Captivating Launch Episode

Creating a captivating launch episode is essential to hook your listeners from the very beginning. Your first episode sets the tone for your entire podcast and can make or break the success of your show. So, how do you craft an episode that captivates your audience and leaves them eagerly waiting for more? Let's dive into the process of turning your podcast idea into an engaging and memorable debut.

First, start by outlining the structure and format of your launch episode. Consider what kind of introduction you want to have, how you'll introduce yourself and your podcast, and what topics or themes you'll cover. This will help you stay organized and ensure a smooth flow throughout the episode.

Next, focus on storytelling. Think about the narrative arc of your episode and how you can create a compelling story that engages your listeners. Begin with a captivating hook that grabs their attention right from the start. This could be a personal anecdote, an intriguing question, or a thought-provoking statement. By capturing their interest, you'll ensure that they stay tuned in for the entire episode.

When it comes to content, be intentional about delivering value to your listeners. Whether it's sharing valuable insights, providing actionable tips, or entertaining them with engaging stories, make sure every minute of your episode adds value and keeps them coming back for more.

Consider incorporating interviews or guest appearances in your launch episode. Bringing in experts or interesting personalities can add variety and depth to your content, making it more compelling and engaging for your audience. If you do include guests, ensure that their contributions are relevant to the overall theme of your podcast and provide valuable insights for your listeners.

Don't forget about production quality. Invest in good equipment, ensure clear audio quality, and edit your episode to remove any unnecessary pauses or distractions. A polished and professional-sounding episode will not only make a good impression on your audience but also keep them engaged and wanting more.

In addition to storytelling and content, think about the overall tone and style of your podcast. What is the personality of your show? Are you going for a conversational and casual vibe, or do you prefer a more formal and informative approach? Think about your target audience and what tone would resonate best with them.

Remember, your launch episode is an opportunity to showcase your podcast's unique value proposition. What sets your podcast apart from others in your niche? What can your listeners expect to gain from tuning in? Highlight these unique aspects in your episode to entice your audience and keep them engaged.

Lastly, end your episode with a strong call-to-action. Encourage your listeners to subscribe, leave a review, or share your podcast with their friends and networks. Building a loyal and engaged audience is crucial for the success of your podcast, and these calls-to-action will help drive growth and word-of-mouth promotion.

Crafting a captivating launch episode requires careful planning, attention to detail, and a deep understanding of your target audience. By creating a compelling narrative, delivering valuable content, and showcasing your podcast's unique value proposition, you can captivate your listeners and leave them eagerly awaiting your next episode. With these strategies in mind, you're well on your way to creating a memorable podcast debut that will keep your audience coming back for more.

Make Your Voice Heard: Submitting Your Podcast to Directories

You've created an amazing podcast with captivating content, and now it's time to make your voice heard by submitting your podcast to directories. Submitting to directories is a crucial step in reaching a wider audience and gaining recognition in the podcasting world. So, let's dive into the process and make sure your podcast gets the exposure it deserves.

First, it's important to understand what podcast directories are and why they are important. Podcast directories are platforms that house a vast collection of podcasts, making it easier for listeners to discover and access new shows. Think of directories like the Yellow Pages of podcasts, where listeners can browse and search for shows based on their interests. Some popular podcast directories include Apple Podcasts, Spotify, Google Podcasts, and Stitcher.

The first and most important step in submitting your podcast to directories is to ensure that you have a well-designed and properly formatted RSS feed. An RSS feed is like a pipeline that delivers your podcast episodes to various directories. Make sure your RSS feed includes all the necessary information, such as your show's title, description, episode titles, release dates, and artwork. This information will help directories categorize and display your podcast accurately.

Once your RSS feed is in order, it's time to start submitting to directories. Begin with the biggest and most popular directories, such as Apple Podcasts. Apple Podcasts is the largest directory, with millions of active users. To submit your podcast to Apple

Podcasts, you'll need an Apple ID and access to iTunes Connect. Follow the submission guidelines provided by Apple, and once your podcast is approved, it will be available on Apple Podcasts for listeners around the world.

In addition to Apple Podcasts, there are other directories you should consider submitting to. Spotify is a popular streaming platform that has seen significant growth in the podcasting space. Spotify allows podcasters to submit their shows through their podcast hosting platform or via direct submission. Google Podcasts is another important directory, especially for Android users. Submitting your podcast to Google Podcasts can increase your visibility and reach a wider audience.

Stitcher is another directory that shouldn't be overlooked. It's a widely used platform with a dedicated and engaged user base. Submitting your podcast to Stitcher can help you connect with listeners who may not be using other directories. Remember to check if there are any specific submission requirements for each directory and ensure that your podcast meets their guidelines.

Once you've submitted your podcast to the major directories, don't stop there. Explore other directories that cater to your specific niche or target audience. There are directories focused on genres like true crime, business, or health and wellness. Submitting to these niche directories can help you reach a more targeted audience who are already interested in your content.

It's important to note that each directory has its own submission process and timeframe for approval. Some directories may take a few days to review and approve your podcast, while others may take a few weeks. Be patient and regularly check your email for updates from the directories. Once your podcast is approved, you'll receive a confirmation email with instructions on how to manage your podcast listing and track its performance.

Submitting your podcast to directories is just the beginning. To maximize your reach, consider promoting your podcast through social media, your website, and by reaching out to relevant influencers or media outlets. Building an engaged community of listeners is crucial for the success of your podcast, so be proactive in promoting and engaging with your audience.

Remember, submitting your podcast to directories is an essential step in making your voice heard. It's a way to connect with a wider audience, gain recognition, and establish your podcast in the podcasting landscape. So, take the time to research, follow the submission guidelines, and get your podcast out there for the world to discover and enjoy.

10 The Ultimate Guide to Growing Your Podcast Audience

In order to reach a wider audience and make an impact with your podcast, you need to actively work on growing your audience. In this comprehensive guide, we will cover everything you need to know about leveraging social media, engaging with your listener community, collaborating with other podcasters, and encouraging reviews and ratings. By implementing these strategies, you will be well on your way to increasing your podcast's reach and building a dedicated fan base.

Unlocking the Power of Social Media for Podcast Growth

In today's digital age, social media has become a powerful tool for connecting with others and sharing information. And as a podcaster, it can be a game-changer when it comes to growing your audience. Unlocking the power of social media for podcast growth is all about leveraging its reach and influence to promote your show and connect with potential listeners.

One of the first steps in harnessing social media's power is to establish a strong presence on popular platforms like Facebook, TikTok, X, Instagram, and LinkedIn. Each platform has its own unique features and audience, so it's important to tailor your content to fit each one. Share teasers or snippets of your podcast episodes, behind-the-scenes footage, or even create short video clips to engage and entice your followers.

But simply having a presence on social media isn't enough. To truly unlock its power, you need to actively engage with your audience. Respond to comments and messages, ask for feedback or suggestions, and start conversations around topics related to your podcast. This will not only help you build a loyal fan base but also provide valuable insights and ideas for future episodes.

Another key strategy for social media growth is to collaborate with influencers or industry experts in your niche. By partnering with others who have a large following, you can tap into their audience and gain exposure to new potential listeners. This can be done through guest appearances on their podcasts, joint promotions, or even cross-promoting each other's content on social media. Collaborations like these can help you expand your reach and attract new listeners who are interested in your podcast's niche.

Lastly, don't forget about the power of hashtags and keywords. Research popular hashtags or keywords in your niche and incorporate them into your social media posts. This will make it easier for people who are interested in your podcast's topic to find your content and potentially become new subscribers. Additionally, consider participating in relevant X chats or Facebook groups to further engage with your target audience.

Unlocking the power of social media for podcast growth requires time, effort, and creativity. But by leveraging its reach, engaging with your audience, collaborating with others, and utilizing hashtags and keywords, you can significantly increase your podcast's visibility and attract a larger audience. So, don't underestimate the power of social media – it's a game-changer for podcasters who are looking to grow their audience and make a lasting impact in their industry.

The Art of Engaging with Your Podcast Listener Community

Building a strong and engaged podcast listener community is not just about creating great content. It's about cultivating a connection with your audience, fostering a sense of belonging, and creating an environment where your listeners feel heard and valued. Engaging with your podcast listener community is an art, and it requires effort and intentionality. Here are some strategies to help you master the art of engaging with your podcast listener community.

First and foremost, make it a priority to actively respond to comments, messages, and feedback from your listeners. Take the time to acknowledge their thoughts and opinions, and show genuine appreciation for their support. By responding to their comments, you not only make them feel seen and heard, but you also create a dialogue that can deepen their connection with your podcast.

Another way to engage with your listener community is to create opportunities for them to participate in your podcast. Consider hosting live Q&A sessions or inviting listeners to submit questions or topic suggestions for future episodes. This not only encourages engagement but also gives your listeners a sense of ownership and involvement in your podcast. By incorporating their ideas and perspectives into your content, you make them feel like valued contributors to your podcast.

In addition to responding to comments and involving your listeners, consider creating a space for your community to connect with each other. This can be in the form of a private Facebook group or an online forum where your listeners can interact with one another, share their thoughts, and discuss the topics covered in your podcast. By facilitating these connections, you foster a sense of community and create a space for your listeners to engage with your content on a deeper level.

Don't forget to leverage the power of social media to engage with your listener community as well. Share snippets or quotes from your episodes and encourage your listeners to share their thoughts or experiences related to the topic. Create polls or surveys to gather feedback and involve your audience in decision-making processes. By incorporating your listeners' voices and opinions into your social media strategy, you make them feel like an integral part of your podcast.

Remember, engaging with your podcast listener community is not a one-way street. It's about creating a meaningful and reciprocal relationship where both you and your listeners benefit. By actively responding to their comments, involving them in your podcast, creating a space for them to connect with each other, and leveraging social media, you can cultivate a thriving listener community that is invested in your podcast and eager to support your growth.

So, take the time to master the art of engaging with your podcast listener community. It may require some trial and error, but the effort will be well worth it.

Successful Collaboration with Other Podcasters: A Strategy to Expand your Audience

Collaborating with other podcasters is a powerful strategy for growing your podcast audience and expanding your reach. By joining forces with other podcasters in your niche or industry, you can tap into their established audience and gain exposure to new potential listeners. The key to successful collaboration lies in finding the right partners and implementing effective strategies.

One way to collaborate with other podcasters is through guest appearances on each other's shows. By appearing as a guest on another podcaster's show, you have the opportunity to share your expertise, reach a new audience, and showcase your podcast to their listeners. This can lead to a significant increase in your own audience and provide a boost in credibility within your niche. Additionally, inviting other podcasters to be guests on your show allows you to introduce your listeners to new voices and perspectives, adding value to your content and keeping your audience engaged.

Another effective strategy is to collaborate on joint episodes or projects. This could involve hosting a live event together, creating a co-produced episode, or even launching a limited series or podcast network. By combining your resources, skills, and audiences, you can create content that is unique, compelling, and mutually beneficial. This not only expands your reach but also adds variety and excitement to your podcast, attracting new listeners who may be intrigued by the collaboration.

Cross-promotion is another powerful collaboration strategy. This involves promoting each other's podcasts or content on social media, newsletters, and other marketing channels. By sharing your podcast with another podcaster's audience, you can leverage their credibility and trust to attract new listeners who may be interested in your content. It's a win-win situation where both parties benefit from the exposure and increased audience reach.

When collaborating with other podcasters, it's important

to choose partners who align with your podcast's values, target audience, and niche. Look for podcasters whose content complements yours and whose audience is likely to be interested in what you have to offer. Building relationships with like-minded podcasters can lead to long-term partnerships and ongoing collaborations that benefit both parties.

Successful collaboration with other podcasters requires open communication, mutual respect, and a willingness to support each other's growth. It's not just about promoting your own podcast, but also about creating a network and community of podcasters who support and uplift each other. By collaborating with others, you not only expand your audience but also become part of a larger podcasting community where you can learn, share insights, and foster meaningful connections.

The Importance of Encouraging Reviews and Ratings for Your Podcast

As a podcaster, you pour your heart and soul into creating high-quality content for your audience. You want your podcast to be impactful and resonate with listeners, but how do you know if you're making a difference? That's where reviews and ratings come in.

Encouraging reviews and ratings for your podcast is essential for several reasons. First and foremost, they provide valuable feedback and insights into what your listeners enjoy and what they want to hear more of. Reviews and ratings give you a direct line of communication with your audience, allowing you to understand their needs and preferences better. By taking their feedback to heart, you can continuously improve your podcast and tailor your content to meet their expectations.

But reviews and ratings are more than just feedback; they also serve as social proof for potential new listeners. When someone is searching for a new podcast to listen to, they often rely on reviews and ratings to gauge whether a podcast is worth their time. Positive reviews and high ratings can make your podcast stand out from the crowd and attract new listeners. It's like a stamp of approval that reassures potential listeners that your podcast is worth checking out.

Encouraging reviews and ratings also helps with discoverability. Many podcast platforms use algorithms to determine which podcasts to recommend to users. Reviews and ratings play a significant role in these algorithms. The more positive reviews and high ratings your podcast has, the more likely it is to be featured and recommended to new listeners. It's a way to increase your visibility and reach a broader audience.

So how do you go about encouraging reviews and ratings for your podcast? One of the most effective strategies is simply asking your listeners to leave a review or rating. Make it a part of your podcast outro or mention it in your show notes. Explain the importance of reviews and how they can help your podcast grow. You can also offer incentives, such as entering listeners into a giveaway or providing exclusive bonus content for those who leave a review.

Additionally, make it as easy as possible for listeners to leave reviews and ratings. Provide clear instructions on how to do so on different podcast platforms and direct them to leave reviews on platforms where it matters most for your podcast's visibility.

Remember, reviews and ratings are not just numbers or comments; they are powerful tools that can help you understand your audience better, attract new listeners, and increase your podcast's visibility. So don't be afraid to ask for reviews and encourage your audience to share their thoughts. It's a win-win situation where both you and your listeners benefit.

Practical Tips and Tricks for Podcast Promotion

So you've created an amazing podcast and now you're ready to promote it to the world. But where do you start? Here are some practical tips and tricks for podcast promotion that will help you get your show in front of more listeners.

First, make sure your podcast is available on all major podcast platforms. This includes platforms like Apple Podcasts, Spotify, Google Podcasts, and Stitcher. The more places your podcast is available, the easier it will be for potential listeners to find and subscribe to it.

Next, optimize your podcast's metadata. This includes your podcast title, description, and episode titles. Use relevant keywords in your metadata to help improve your podcast's visibility in search results. Think about what people might be searching for when looking for podcasts in your niche and incorporate those keywords into your metadata.

Another great way to promote your podcast is by leveraging your existing network. Reach out to friends, family, and colleagues and ask them to listen to and share your podcast with their networks. Word of mouth is a powerful tool, and having people you know vouch for your podcast can help attract new listeners.

Consider creating a podcast trailer to entice potential listeners. A trailer is a short preview of your podcast that gives listeners a taste of what to expect. It's a great way to generate excitement and get people interested in your show. Share your trailer on social media, your website, and in any other promotional materials you have.

Utilize social media to promote your podcast. Create eye-catching graphics and share them on platforms like Facebook, TikTok, X, and Instagram. Use relevant hashtags to increase the visibility of your posts. Engage with your followers by responding to comments and messages, and ask them to share your podcast with their networks.

Collaborate with other content creators in your niche.

This could include guest appearances on other podcasts, writing guest blog posts, or participating in interviews. By collaborating with others, you can tap into their audience and gain exposure to new potential listeners.

Consider running contests or giveaways to incentivize listeners to promote your podcast. This could include giving away merchandise, offering exclusive bonus content, or even hosting live events or meetups. Contests and giveaways can generate buzz and excitement around your podcast, and they encourage your existing listeners to spread the word.

Finally, don't forget about the power of email marketing. Build an email list and send regular updates and reminders about your podcast to your subscribers. This keeps your podcast top of mind and encourages repeat listens and recommendations.

By implementing these practical tips and tricks, you'll be well on your way to promoting your podcast and growing your audience.

The Long-Term Benefits of Growing Your Podcast Audience

Growing your podcast audience isn't just about gaining more listeners in the short term. It has long-term benefits that can help take your podcast to the next level and solidify your place in the podcasting industry.

One of the key long-term benefits of growing your podcast audience is increased visibility and recognition. As your audience grows, more people will discover your podcast and recognize your name. This can open up opportunities for collaborations, sponsorships, and other partnerships that can further enhance the success of your podcast. Being known and respected in your niche can also lead to speaking engagements, media features, and other opportunities to share your expertise and expand your reach.

Another long-term benefit of growing your podcast audience is increased credibility. As your audience grows, so does your credibility in the eyes of potential listeners. People are more likely to trust a podcast that has a large and engaged audience, as it serves as social proof that your content is valuable and worth their time. This credibility can attract new listeners who may have been hesitant to give your podcast a chance before.

With a larger audience, you also have the opportunity to generate more revenue from your podcast. Advertisers and sponsors are more likely to invest in podcasts with a significant and engaged audience, as they see it as a valuable platform to reach their target market. Growing your podcast audience can open up new monetization opportunities, whether through sponsorships, merchandise sales, or even paid subscriptions.

Additionally, growing your podcast audience can lead to a stronger and more supportive community around your podcast. As your audience grows, you'll have more opportunities to connect with your listeners, hear their feedback, and build meaningful relationships. This community can become a valuable resource, providing support, ideas, and even helping with the promotion of your podcast. A dedicated and engaged listener community can create a sense of belonging and loyalty, and can be a powerful driving force behind the success of your podcast.

In conclusion, growing your podcast audience has numerous long-term benefits that can help elevate your podcast to new heights. Increased visibility, credibility, revenue opportunities, and a strong listener community are just a few of the rewards that come with growing your audience. So, put in the time and effort to implement the strategies outlined in this guide, and watch your podcast thrive and make a lasting impact in the podcasting industry.

11 Making Money from Your Passion

For many podcasters, creating and sharing content is a labor of love. It's a way to express their passions, share their knowledge, and engage with a community of listeners. But what if you could turn that passion into a source of income? With the growing popularity of podcasting, there are now more opportunities than ever to monetize your show and make a profit from doing what you love. In this guide, we'll explore different revenue streams for podcasters, from sponsorships and partnerships to setting up a Patreon or membership program. Whether you're a seasoned podcaster or just starting out, this post will provide valuable insights and tips on how to make money from your passion through your podcast.

Understanding the Different Revenue Streams for Your Podcast

As a podcaster, there are various revenue streams you can explore to monetize your show and turn your passion into a profitable venture. Understanding these different revenue streams is key to creating a successful and sustainable podcasting business.

One of the most common revenue streams for podcasters is sponsorships and partnerships. This involves collaborating with brands or companies that align with your podcast's niche and values. Sponsors typically pay to have their products or services promoted on your show, either through ad spots or mentions during episodes. Partnering with brands that resonate with your audience can be mutually beneficial, providing you with financial support while also giving your listeners access to products or services they may find valuable.

Another revenue stream to consider is setting up a Patreon or membership program. These platforms allow your listeners to become patrons or members by subscribing to exclusive content or perks. This creates a sense of community and loyalty among your audience, as they feel more connected and invested in your show. Offering bonus episodes, behind-the-scenes content, or early access to episodes are just a few examples of the exclusive content you can provide to your patrons. In return, they pay a recurring fee, providing you with a steady stream of income.

Beyond sponsorships and membership programs, there are additional revenue streams to explore. You can sell merchandise related to your podcast, such as t-shirts, mugs, or stickers. This not only generates additional income, but also serves as a form of promotion as your fans proudly display their support for your show. Additionally, you can offer consulting or coaching services to share your expertise with other aspiring podcasters or individuals in your podcast's niche.

Diversifying your revenue streams is essential for long-term success. By leveraging multiple avenues, you reduce the risk of relying solely on one source of income. It also allows you to cater to different audience preferences and demographics. However, it's important to strike a balance and not overwhelm your listeners with excessive ads or too many paid offerings. Your primary focus should always be on creating valuable and engaging content for your audience.

Understanding the different revenue streams available to podcasters opens up opportunities for growth and sustainability. It allows you to transform your passion into a viable business, where you can continue to create content that resonates with your audience while also generating income. By exploring sponsorships, membership programs, merchandise sales, and additional services, you can build a profitable podcasting business and further establish yourself as a leader in your niche. So, don't be afraid to explore these revenue streams and start making money from your podcast today.

How to Find and Secure Sponsorships and Partnerships

Finding and securing sponsorships and partnerships for your podcast can be a great way to monetize your show and generate a steady stream of income. However, it can be a daunting task if you're not sure where to start. In this section, we'll discuss some effective strategies to help you find and secure sponsorships and partnerships for your podcast.

First and foremost, it's important to have a clear understanding of your podcast's niche, target audience, and value proposition. Knowing your audience demographics, interests, and what sets your podcast apart from others will make it easier to find sponsors and partners that align with your content and values. Take the time to research brands and companies that have a similar target audience or share a common interest with your podcast.

One effective way to find potential sponsors and partners is to network within your niche or industry. Attend industry events, join relevant online communities or forums, and engage with influencers and experts in your field. Building relationships and connections with other podcasters, industry professionals, and potential sponsors can open doors to partnership opportunities. Consider reaching out to companies or brands that you admire or have mentioned on your show and express your interest in working together.

Another strategy is to leverage your existing audience and engagement metrics. Brands are more likely to consider partnering with you if you have an engaged and loyal audience. Compile data such as your podcast's download numbers, social media following, and engagement rates to showcase your reach and influence. Consider creating a media kit that includes information about your podcast, target audience, engagement metrics, and sponsorship opportunities.

When reaching out to potential sponsors and partners, personalize your pitch to demonstrate that you've done your research and genuinely believe in their products or services. Highlight the benefits of collaborating with your podcast, such as reaching a highly targeted audience or aligning with your podcast's values and mission. Be clear about what you can offer in terms of promotional opportunities, whether it's ad spots, mentions during episodes, or other creative integrations.

Lastly, it's essential to maintain transparency and open communication with your sponsors and partners. Clearly outline expectations, deliverables, and the terms of the partnership in a written agreement or contract. Regularly evaluate the effectiveness of the partnership and provide reports or analytics to demonstrate the value you're bringing to the table. Nurturing these relationships can lead to long-term sponsorships and partnerships.

Establishing a Successful Patreon or Membership Program

If you're looking for a way to generate a steady stream of income from your podcast, setting up a Patreon or membership program can be a highly effective strategy. These platforms allow your loyal listeners to become patrons or members by subscribing to exclusive content or perks. Not only does this create a sense of community and loyalty among your audience, but it also provides you with a consistent source of income.

To establish a successful Patreon or membership program, it's important to start by clearly defining what exclusive content or perks you will offer to your patrons. This can include bonus episodes, behind-the-scenes content, early access to episodes, or even merchandise discounts. The key is to provide something of value that your listeners can't get anywhere else. This will entice them to become patrons and continue supporting your podcast.

Next, you'll need to decide on the pricing structure for your Patreon or membership program. Consider offering different tiers or levels of membership, each with its own set of benefits. This allows your audience to choose the level of support that aligns with their budget and preferences. Offering a range of options can attract a wider range of patrons and increase your overall revenue.

Once you've established your Patreon or membership program, it's important to promote it consistently across your podcast and other platforms. Clearly communicate the benefits of becoming a patron and explain how their support directly contributes to the sustainability of your show. Utilize social media, email newsletters, and in-episode mentions to remind your listeners about the perks and exclusive content they can access by becoming a member.

Regularly engaging with your patrons is another crucial aspect of a successful Patreon or membership program. Take the time to respond to comments and messages, show appreciation for their support, and seek feedback on what type of content they would like to see more of. This not only strengthens the sense of community among your patrons but also ensures that you are providing them with content they find valuable.

Lastly, continue to evaluate and iterate on your Patreon or membership program as your podcast grows. Pay attention to which benefits are resonating with your patrons and consider adding or adjusting perks based on their feedback. This ongoing refinement will help keep your program fresh and engaging, leading to higher retention rates and increased revenue.

By establishing a successful Patreon or membership program, you can create a dedicated community of supporters who not only enjoy your content but also want to financially contribute to its continuation. With the right approach, this revenue stream can provide you with a stable source of income while fostering a deeper connection with your audience. So don't hesitate to explore the potential of Patreon and membership programs to monetize your podcast and turn your passion into a profitable venture.

Tips and Tricks for Consistently Increasing Your Podcast Revenue

Looking to increase your podcast revenue? Here are some tips and tricks to help you consistently grow your income and monetize your passion.

1. Focus on audience growth: One of the most effective ways to increase your podcast revenue is by expanding your audience. Concentrate on growing your listenership by promoting your show across different platforms and engaging with your audience through social media. Encourage your current listeners to share your episodes and leave reviews, as positive word-of-mouth can attract new listeners and potential sponsors.

2. Optimize your monetization strategies: Continuously assess and optimize your monetization strategies to maximize your income potential. Experiment with different ad formats and sponsorship opportunities to find what works best for your audience. Monitor listener feedback and engagement metrics to gauge the effectiveness of your monetization efforts and make adjustments accordingly.

3. Offer additional paid content: Consider offering additional paid content to your audience to supplement your main podcast episodes. This can include bonus episodes, in-depth interviews, or exclusive behind-the-scenes content. By providing additional value to your listeners, you can create additional revenue streams

while also deepening their engagement and loyalty.

4. Utilize affiliate marketing: Affiliate marketing can be a lucrative way to generate income from your podcast. Partner with companies or brands that align with your podcast's niche and promote their products or services through unique affiliate links. Whenever a listener makes a purchase through your link, you earn a commission. Be transparent about your affiliate relationships and only promote products or services that you genuinely believe in.

5. Seek out speaking engagements: Capitalize on your expertise and podcasting success by seeking out speaking engagements or panel opportunities. Many events and conferences are willing to pay experienced podcasters to share their insights and knowledge with attendees. Not only does this provide an additional revenue stream, but it also helps to establish you as an authority in your podcasting niche.

6. Engage with your audience: Building a strong and loyal community around your podcast can lead to increased revenue opportunities. Take the time to engage with your audience through social media, emails, or even virtual meet-ups. This not only strengthens the connection with your listeners but can also lead to opportunities for merchandise sales, live events, or crowdfunding campaigns.

7. Stay up to date with industry trends: The podcasting industry is constantly evolving, and it's essential to stay

up to date with the latest trends and best practices. Attend industry events, listen to other podcasts in your niche, and stay connected with podcasting communities. By staying informed, you can identify new revenue opportunities, adapt to changes, and position yourself as a leader in the industry.

Consistently increasing your podcast revenue takes time, effort, and a willingness to adapt.

Case Studies of Successful Monetization Strategies in Podcasting

Podcasting has become an incredibly popular medium, attracting a diverse range of creators and listeners. With the increasing popularity of podcasting, more and more podcasters are looking for ways to monetize their shows and turn their passion into a profitable venture. To inspire and guide you on your monetization journey, let's explore some real-life case studies of successful podcasters who have found creative and effective ways to generate revenue from their podcasts.

One such case study is the podcast "The Moth," which is a storytelling podcast that features real people sharing their personal stories on stage. The podcast has been able to monetize through live events and ticket sales. They organize live storytelling events in different cities, where podcast listeners and fans can attend and enjoy the experience firsthand. By selling tickets to these events, "The Moth" is able to generate revenue while also providing a unique and immersive experience to their audience.

Another case study is the podcast "The GaryVee Audio Experience" by entrepreneur and author Gary Vaynerchuk. GaryVee has successfully monetized his podcast through sponsorships and partnerships. He has partnered with various brands that align with his podcast's target audience and values. Through ad spots and mentions during episodes, he promotes these brands and earns revenue from sponsorships. This strategy allows GaryVee to provide valuable content to his listeners while also generating income from sponsorships.

The "Joe Rogan Experience" podcast, hosted by comedian Joe Rogan, has found success through a combination of sponsorships, merchandise sales, and live events. Joe Rogan has built a loyal and engaged audience over the years, and he has been able to leverage that by selling merchandise such as t-shirts, hats, and posters. Additionally, he organizes live events where fans can come and see him perform live or engage in discussions with guests. By diversifying his revenue streams, Joe Rogan has been able to generate significant income from his podcast.

These case studies highlight the importance of diversifying revenue streams and finding creative ways to monetize your podcast. Whether it's through live events, sponsorships, merchandise sales, or a combination of strategies, there are various paths to monetization. It's crucial to understand your audience and find revenue streams that align with your podcast's niche and values. By studying successful podcasters like "The Moth," GaryVee, and Joe Rogan, you can gain valuable insights and inspiration for your own monetization journey.

Common Mistakes to Avoid When Monetizing Your Podcast

Monetizing your podcast can be an exciting journey, but it's important to navigate it carefully to avoid common mistakes that can hinder your success. Here are some key mistakes to avoid when monetizing your podcast:

1. Neglecting your audience: Your audience is the backbone of your podcast and should always be your top priority. Avoid overwhelming them with excessive ads or paid offerings that don't provide value. Always prioritize creating high-quality, engaging content that resonates with your audience. Remember, happy listeners are more likely to become loyal patrons and contribute to your revenue streams.

2. Lack of transparency: Transparency is key when it comes to monetizing your podcast. Be upfront with your audience about any sponsorships, partnerships, or paid content you offer. Clearly disclose any financial arrangements and maintain trust by only endorsing products or services you genuinely believe in. Building an honest and transparent relationship with your

audience will foster loyalty and credibility.

3. Failing to diversify revenue streams: Relying solely on one source of income can be risky. It's important to diversify your revenue streams to ensure a stable and sustainable income. Explore different avenues such as sponsorships, membership programs, merchandise sales, and affiliate marketing. By diversifying, you can better adapt to changes in the industry and cater to different audience preferences.

4. Lack of consistency: Consistency is crucial when monetizing your podcast. Avoid irregular release schedules or gaps in content production. This can lead to a loss of audience engagement and potential revenue. Establish a consistent schedule and deliver high-quality content consistently to maintain the interest and support of your listeners.

5. Overlooking analytics and data: Analytics and data can provide valuable insights into the effectiveness of your monetization strategies. Monitor your download numbers, listener demographics, and engagement rates to evaluate the success of your revenue streams. This data can help you make informed decisions and optimize your strategies for better results.

6. Ignoring feedback and not adapting: Your audience's feedback is a valuable resource for improving your podcast and monetization strategies. Listen to their feedback, whether it's through comments, reviews, or surveys, and use it to refine your offerings. Be open to

adapting your approach and experimenting with different strategies to better serve your audience and maximize your revenue potential.

7. Unrealistic expectations: Monetizing your podcast takes time and effort. Don't expect instant success or significant revenue overnight. Building a sustainable and profitable podcasting business requires dedication, consistency, and a long-term mindset. Set realistic expectations, focus on continuous growth, and celebrate the small milestones along the way.

12 Interpreting Podcast Analytics and Feedback

As podcasting continues to grow in popularity, it has become increasingly important for podcasters to understand and utilize the data available through analytics and listener feedback. These tools can provide valuable insights into your audience and their listening habits, helping you tailor your content and reach a wider audience. In this chapter, we will explore how to interpret podcast analytics and gather listener feedback, and how to use this information to adjust your podcasting strategy for success.

Demystifying Podcast Analytics: The Why and the How

Podcast analytics may sound intimidating, but they are an invaluable tool for podcasters. Understanding the why and the how of podcast analytics can provide you with valuable insights into your audience and help you make informed decisions about your content and strategy. So, let's demystify podcast analytics and explore why they are so important and how you can leverage them to take your podcast to the next level.

Firstly, why should you care about podcast analytics? Well, simply put, they give you a glimpse into the behaviors and preferences of your listeners. Podcasting is a unique medium because it allows you to reach a wide and diverse audience, but without analytics, you would be shooting in the dark. Analytics help you answer crucial questions like: Who is listening to your podcast? How long are they listening? Where are they tuning in from? By understanding these metrics, you can gain valuable insights into the demographic makeup of your audience and tailor your content to their preferences.

One of the most important metrics in podcast analytics is the number of downloads and listens. This metric gives you a general sense of your podcast's popularity and reach. Additionally, tracking the average listen duration can help you identify which episodes are resonating with your audience and which may need some adjustments. For example, if you notice a significant drop-off in listens halfway through an episode, it may be a sign that the content is not engaging enough or that the episode is too long.

Another crucial aspect of podcast analytics is audience retention. This metric tells you how many listeners are sticking around for the entire episode versus dropping off at various points. By examining audience retention, you can identify patterns and trends that indicate which parts of your episodes are most engaging and which may need improvement. Perhaps you notice a dip in retention during a specific segment or topic – this can be a signal that your audience is less interested in that particular content and that you should consider adjusting or even removing it.

Geographic data is also a valuable component of podcast analytics. It allows you to see where your listeners are tuning in from, giving you insights into your podcast's global reach. This information can be particularly helpful if you have sponsors or advertisers who are interested in reaching specific geographic regions. By understanding your listeners' locations, you can pitch your podcast to potential advertisers with confidence and attract partnerships that align with your audience's interests.

Beyond the quantitative metrics, podcast analytics can also provide qualitative feedback. Through reviews and ratings, listeners offer valuable insights into what they love about your podcast and areas where you can improve. Reviews can be a goldmine of feedback, giving you a sense of what resonates with your audience and what they want more of. Paying attention to reviews and engaging with your listeners' feedback can help you build a loyal community and continuously refine your content.

Sourcing Valuable Insights: The Importance of Listener Feedback

Podcast analytics are an essential tool for understanding your audience, but they only provide part of the picture. To truly get a complete understanding of your podcast and its impact, you need to gather listener feedback. Listener feedback goes beyond the numbers and allows you to hear directly from your audience, gaining valuable insights into their preferences, interests, and suggestions for improvement.

So why is listener feedback so important? Well, for starters, it helps you understand the impact your podcast is having on your audience. Are they finding value in your content? Are they entertained? Are they learning something new? Listener feedback can help you gauge how well you are meeting your listeners' expectations and identify areas where you can improve.

Listener feedback also helps you establish a connection with your audience. When your listeners take the time to provide feedback, they are showing that they are invested in your podcast and that they value your content. By acknowledging and engaging with their feedback, you can strengthen that connection and build a loyal community of listeners.

But how do you gather listener feedback? There are several ways you can do this. One of the most common ways is through reviews and ratings on podcast platforms. Encourage your listeners to leave reviews and ratings by mentioning it at the end of each episode or by including a call-to-action in your show notes. These reviews can provide valuable insights into what your listeners love about your podcast and areas where you can improve.

Another way to gather feedback is through social

media. Engage with your listeners on platforms like TikTok, X, Instagram, and Facebook, and encourage them to share their thoughts, questions, and suggestions. Social media provides a more interactive space for your audience to engage with you and for you to gather feedback in real-time.

You can also consider creating a dedicated feedback form on your podcast's website or sending out surveys to your listeners via email. These methods allow you to ask specific questions and gather more detailed feedback on particular aspects of your podcast. For example, you can ask your listeners which topics they enjoy the most, what format they prefer, or if there are any guests they would like to see on your show.

When gathering listener feedback, it's important to approach it with an open mind and a willingness to learn. Your audience's perspectives and opinions may differ from your own, and that's okay. Remember that your podcast is ultimately for your listeners, and their feedback can help you shape and refine your content to better serve their needs.

Once you have gathered listener feedback, take the time to analyze and reflect on it. Look for common themes or patterns in the feedback to identify areas where you can make improvements. Keep in mind that not all feedback will be actionable or align with your podcast's goals and vision, and that's okay too. Use your judgment and make changes that will enhance your podcast while staying true to your unique voice and style.

Translating Data Into Action: Adapting Your Podcast Strategy

Now that you have a deeper understanding of podcast analytics and listener feedback, it's time to put that data into action and adapt your podcast strategy. By using the insights gathered from analytics and feedback, you can make informed decisions that will help improve the quality of your podcast and better serve your audience.

The first step in translating data into action is to analyze the trends and patterns that emerge from your podcast analytics. Look for common themes in the data and identify areas where improvements can be made. For example, if you notice that episodes on a specific topic consistently receive higher listen durations and retention rates, consider incorporating more content on that topic into future episodes. Conversely, if certain segments or topics consistently result in lower engagement, it may be worth reevaluating or removing them to keep your audience engaged throughout the entire episode.

In addition to quantitative metrics, listener feedback plays a crucial role in adapting your podcast strategy. Pay close attention to the feedback you receive, both positive and negative. Positive feedback can reinforce what you are doing well and provide insight into what resonates with your audience. Take note of the aspects that are particularly well-received and consider incorporating more of them into your future episodes.

Negative feedback, on the other hand, can be equally valuable. While it can be disheartening to receive criticism, it provides an opportunity for growth and improvement. Consider negative feedback as constructive criticism and use it as a catalyst for change. Look for recurring themes or patterns in the feedback and identify areas where adjustments can be made. It's important to remember that not all feedback will be actionable, and you should use your judgment to make changes that align with your podcast's goals and vision.

Once you have analyzed both the analytics and listener feedback, it's time to implement the changes and adapt your podcast strategy. This can include anything from adjusting the format of your episodes to incorporating new topics or segments based on listener preferences. Experiment with different ideas and track the impact of these changes through your analytics. Keep an eye on key metrics such as download numbers, listen duration, and audience retention to gauge the success of your adaptations.

It's worth noting that adapting your podcast strategy is an ongoing process. As your audience evolves and your podcast grows, it's important to continue collecting and analyzing data to ensure you are meeting your listeners' needs. Stay open to feedback and be willing to make adjustments along the way. Your podcast should be a reflection of your audience's interests and preferences, so be prepared to iterate and refine your content based on their feedback.

Practical Steps to Improve Based on Analytics and Feedback

Now that you have a deeper understanding of podcast analytics and listener feedback, it's time to take action and use that data to improve your podcast. Here are some practical steps you can take to adapt your podcast strategy based on analytics and feedback:

1. Analyze the data: Start by diving into your podcast analytics and listener feedback. Look for trends and patterns that emerge from the data. Pay attention to metrics like download numbers, listen duration, audience retention, and geographic data. Identify areas where improvements can be made and take note of what is resonating with your audience.

2. Incorporate successful elements: Take note of the aspects of your podcast that are receiving positive feedback and performing well in the analytics. These are the elements that are resonating with your audience and keeping them engaged. Consider incorporating more of these successful elements into your future episodes. Whether it's a specific topic,

format, or segment, giving your audience more of what they love will help you grow your podcast and attract a wider audience.

3. Address areas of improvement: On the flip side, pay attention to negative feedback and areas where the analytics indicate lower engagement. While negative feedback can be tough to receive, it's an opportunity for growth and improvement. Look for recurring themes or patterns in the feedback and identify areas where adjustments can be made. Whether it's the length of your episodes, the pacing, or certain segments, be willing to make changes that align with your listeners' needs and preferences.

4. Experiment and track results: Once you've identified areas for improvement, don't be afraid to experiment and try new things. Incorporate changes based on feedback and analytics and track the impact of these adjustments. Keep an eye on key metrics such as download numbers, listen duration, and audience retention to gauge the success of your adaptations. Be willing to iterate and refine your content based on the data and feedback you receive.

5. Engage with your audience: Encourage ongoing feedback from your listeners and create opportunities for them to engage with you. Use social media platforms like TikTok, X, Instagram, and Facebook to interact with your audience and gather real-time feedback. Consider creating a dedicated feedback form

on your podcast's website or sending out surveys to your listeners via email. By actively seeking feedback and engaging with your audience, you can continue to refine your content and better serve their needs.

6. Stay open to learning and evolving: Remember that adapting your podcast strategy is an ongoing process. As your audience evolves and your podcast grows, it's important to continue collecting and analyzing data to ensure you are meeting your listeners' needs. Stay open to feedback, both positive and negative, and be willing to make adjustments along the way. Your podcast should be a reflection of your audience's interests and preferences, so be prepared to iterate and refine your content based on their feedback.

By taking these practical steps and using analytics and listener feedback as your guide, you can continuously improve the quality of your podcast and better serve your audience. Embrace the clues your listeners are giving you and let their feedback shape and refine your content.

13 The Top Tech Hurdles Podcasters Face

While it may seem like a simple process to record and upload a podcast episode, there are often numerous technical hurdles that podcasters face behind the scenes. These challenges can range from equipment malfunctions to software issues and can significantly impact the production and success of a podcast. In this chapter, we will take a deeper look at the top tech hurdles that podcasters encounter and how to overcome them. So, whether you are a seasoned podcaster or just starting out, keep reading to learn more about troubleshooting and common challenges in the world of podcasting.

Breaking Down the Common Technical Glitches in Podcasting

Podcasting may seem like a straightforward process, but any experienced podcaster will tell you that it often comes with its fair share of technical glitches. From unexpected audio issues to software crashes, these technical hiccups can be frustrating and disruptive to the podcasting workflow. In this section, we will dive into some of the most common technical glitches that podcasters encounter and provide tips on how to overcome them.

One of the most prevalent technical glitches in

podcasting is audio quality problems. This can include background noise, echoes, or muffled voices that can greatly detract from the listening experience. To address this issue, it's essential to invest in high-quality recording equipment and create a conducive recording environment. Consider using a good quality microphone, soundproofing your recording space, and experimenting with different audio editing techniques to enhance the sound quality. Additionally, conducting regular sound checks before recording can help identify any audio issues before they become a problem.

Another common technical glitch is the dreaded software crash. Podcasters often rely on recording and editing software to produce their episodes, and when these programs crash or freeze, it can be incredibly frustrating. To avoid this, make sure you are using the latest version of your chosen software and regularly update it. Additionally, consider using multiple backups and saving your work frequently to prevent losing hours of editing. It's also a good idea to have a backup recording device in case of any software malfunctions during a recording session.

Internet connectivity issues can also cause headaches for podcasters, especially for those who conduct remote interviews or record online. Poor internet connections can lead to lagging audio, dropped calls, and overall poor quality recordings. To minimize the risk of internet-related glitches, it's crucial to have a stable and reliable internet connection. Consider using an ethernet cable for a more stable connection, positioning yourself closer to the router, or even upgrading your internet plan if necessary. Additionally, having a backup recording method, such as a local recording, can help salvage an interview or recording session if the internet connection fails.

Editing and post-production can be a time-consuming process, and one of the common glitches in this stage is losing or corrupting files. This can happen due to computer crashes, file transfer errors, or accidental deletion. To avoid this, it's important to have a reliable file management system in place. Organize your files in a logical and consistent manner, and consider using cloud storage or external hard drives for backup. Additionally, consider implementing an automatic backup system to ensure that your files are continuously protected.

Another technical glitch that podcasters often face is the challenge of podcast hosting and distribution. Once your episode is edited and ready to be shared with the world, you'll need a podcast hosting platform to store and distribute your episodes. However, navigating through different hosting platforms, RSS feeds, and directories can be overwhelming, especially for beginners. To overcome this hurdle, take the time to research and choose a hosting platform that suits your needs. Look for a platform that offers reliable customer support, easy-to-use interface, and seamless distribution to popular podcast directories. Additionally, take advantage of online tutorials and resources that can guide you through the process and answer any questions you may have.

Lastly, compatibility issues can arise when it comes to podcast playback on different devices and platforms. While your podcast may sound great on your computer, it may not have the same quality on other devices or platforms. To ensure compatibility, consider testing your podcast on various devices and platforms to ensure a consistent and high-quality listening experience for your audience. Additionally, it's essential to stay updated with the latest industry standards and specifications for podcasting, as these can change over time.

In conclusion, podcasting comes with its fair share of technical glitches, but with the right knowledge and preparation, these hurdles can be overcome. By investing in quality recording equipment, ensuring a stable internet connection, implementing a robust file management system, and staying updated with the latest industry standards, podcasters can minimize technical glitches and create a seamless and enjoyable listening experience for their audience. So, don't let technical issues discourage you from pursuing your podcasting dreams – embrace these challenges and find innovative solutions to overcome them.

14 How to Avoid Podcast Burnout

The pressure to consistently produce quality content and keep up with the demands of running a podcast can be overwhelming and exhausting. This can lead to a lack of inspiration and motivation, causing many podcasters to give up on their passion. But don't worry. In this chapter, we will discuss some tips and strategies on how to avoid podcast burnout and stay consistently inspired to continue your podcasting journey.

Identifying and Overcoming the Signs of Podcasting Burnout

Podcasting is an incredibly rewarding creative pursuit, but it's not without its challenges. The pressure to consistently produce high-quality content, stay on top of promotion and marketing, and manage the technical aspects of running a podcast can quickly lead to burnout. Burnout is a state of physical and emotional exhaustion that can leave podcasters feeling overwhelmed, uninspired, and even questioning whether it's worth continuing their podcasting journey.

One of the first steps in overcoming podcast burnout is to recognize the signs. It's important to be able to identify when you're feeling burned out so you can take proactive steps to address it. Some common signs of podcasting burnout include:

1. Decreased Motivation: If you find yourself dreading

the thought of recording or editing episodes, or you feel unmotivated to work on your podcast, it may be a sign of burnout. When your passion for podcasting starts to dwindle, it's crucial to take a step back and reassess what's causing this lack of motivation.

2. Creative Block: Burnout can stifle your creativity, making it difficult to come up with new episode ideas or fresh approaches to your content. If you find yourself struggling to generate ideas or feeling stuck in a creative rut, it's time to address the burnout and reignite your creative spark.

3. Physical and Mental Exhaustion: Podcasting requires a lot of energy and effort. If you find yourself constantly tired, experiencing frequent headaches or muscle tension, or feeling mentally drained, it may be a sign that you're pushing yourself too hard and need to take a break.

4. Lack of Enjoyment: When you first started podcasting, it was likely because you enjoyed it. If podcasting starts to feel like a chore or something you're no longer enjoying, it's a clear indicator that burnout is setting in.

Once you've recognized the signs of burnout, it's time to take action and overcome it. Here are some strategies to help you navigate through podcast burnout:

1. Take a Break: Sometimes, the best thing you can do

for yourself and your podcast is to take a break. Step away from podcasting for a short period of time to recharge and refocus. Use this time to engage in activities that bring you joy and inspiration, whether it's reading, traveling, or spending time with loved ones.

2. Reevaluate Your Goals: Burnout can be a sign that you've set unrealistic goals for yourself or have taken on too much. Take a step back and reassess what you want to achieve with your podcast. Are your goals still aligned with your passions and interests? Adjust your goals if needed to ensure they're sustainable and manageable.

3. Seek Support: Don't be afraid to reach out to fellow podcasters or online communities for support and advice. Connecting with others who understand the challenges of podcasting can provide valuable insight, encouragement, and a fresh perspective.

4. Rediscover Your Passion: Take time to reconnect with what initially drew you to podcasting. Remind yourself of the joy and excitement you felt when you first started. Explore new topics or formats that reignite your passion for podcasting.

Podcasting burnout is a common challenge, but it's not insurmountable. By recognizing the signs, taking proactive steps to address burnout, and staying connected to your passion, you can overcome burnout and continue on your podcasting journey with renewed inspiration and motivation. Remember, your podcast is an expression of your creativity and unique voice – take care of yourself, and your podcast will flourish.

Staying Motivated: Techniques to Keep Your Podcast Inspiration Flowing

Staying motivated is key to keeping your podcast inspiration flowing. When the initial excitement wears off and the daily demands of podcasting start to take a toll, it's important to have strategies in place to keep yourself motivated and inspired. Here are some techniques that can help you stay on track and maintain your passion for podcasting:

1. Find your why: Remind yourself of why you started podcasting in the first place. What is the purpose behind your podcast? What impact do you want to make? Understanding your why can help you stay motivated, especially during challenging times. Whether it's to educate, entertain, or inspire your audience, keep your purpose at the forefront of your mind.

2. Set small, achievable goals: Instead of overwhelming yourself with big, long-term goals, break them down into smaller, achievable milestones. By focusing on these smaller goals, you'll have a sense of accomplishment along the way, which can keep you motivated. Celebrate each milestone as you reach it and use it as fuel to keep going.

3. Create a routine: Establishing a consistent routine

can help you stay on track and maintain motivation. Whether it's recording episodes at a specific time each week or dedicating certain days for research and planning, having a routine creates structure and discipline. This routine will help you stay organized and focused on your podcasting goals.

4. Stay inspired through research and learning: Keep yourself engaged and inspired by staying up to date with the latest trends and developments in your niche. Set aside time to research and learn new things related to your podcast topic. This not only keeps your content fresh and relevant but also sparks new ideas and perspectives.

5. Mix up your content: If you find yourself getting bored or uninspired with your current format, try experimenting with different types of content. Incorporate interviews, panel discussions, or solo episodes to add variety and keep your audience engaged. Don't be afraid to think outside the box and try new things. This can reignite your passion and keep your podcasting journey exciting.

6. Seek feedback and engage with your audience: Feedback from your listeners can be incredibly motivating. Encourage your audience to provide feedback, whether through comments, emails, or social media. Engage with your listeners and create a community around your podcast. This interaction can inspire you and give you a sense of purpose and

connection.

7. Take care of yourself: Self-care is crucial when it comes to maintaining motivation and inspiration. Take breaks when you need them and prioritize your mental and physical well-being. Make sure to rest, exercise, and spend time doing activities that bring you joy and recharge your energy. Remember, taking care of yourself is not selfish – it's necessary for sustaining your creativity and passion.

8. Keep a gratitude journal: Cultivating a gratitude practice can shift your perspective and help you appreciate the journey. Take a few moments each day to write down things you're grateful for in relation to your podcasting experience. It could be positive feedback from a listener, a successful episode, or simply the opportunity to share your voice with the world. Focusing on gratitude can keep you motivated and grounded in the joy of podcasting.

By implementing these techniques, you can stay motivated and inspired throughout your podcasting journey. Remember that motivation may ebb and flow, but with the right mindset and strategies, you can overcome challenges and continue to create meaningful content that resonates with your audience. Keep your passion alive and let your unique voice shine through in every episode.

Balancing Ambition and Sustainability in Podcasting

In the world of podcasting, it's easy to get caught up in the excitement and ambition of creating amazing content that captivates listeners. As podcasters, we want to make a mark and leave a lasting impression. However, it's important to find a balance between ambition and sustainability to avoid burnout and maintain a successful podcasting journey.

Ambition is what drives us to dream big and set lofty goals for our podcasts. It's what pushes us to continuously improve our content, reach a larger audience, and make a meaningful impact. But while ambition is important, it's equally important to consider the sustainability of our efforts.

Sustainability refers to the ability to maintain the quality and consistency of our podcasting efforts over the long term. It means finding a rhythm and workflow that allows us to consistently produce high-quality episodes without sacrificing our mental and physical well-being. Balancing ambition and sustainability is crucial to avoid burning out and giving up on our podcasting dreams.

So how do we find this balance? Here are some tips and strategies to help you achieve both ambition and sustainability in your podcasting journey:

1. Set realistic goals: While it's important to have big dreams and aspirations, it's equally important to set realistic goals that are attainable within your available resources and time constraints. Break down your long-term goals into smaller, manageable milestones that

you can work towards. This will not only keep you motivated but also prevent overwhelm and burnout.

2. Prioritize quality over quantity: It's easy to fall into the trap of trying to release episodes on a strict schedule, even if it means sacrificing the quality of your content. Instead, focus on creating valuable and engaging episodes that resonate with your audience. Consistently delivering high-quality content will ultimately lead to more growth and success in the long run.

3. Delegate and outsource: As your podcast grows, you may find it difficult to manage all aspects of podcast production on your own. Consider delegating or outsourcing certain tasks such as editing, show notes writing, or social media management. This will free up your time and energy, allowing you to focus on creating great content and maintaining your motivation.

4. Practice self-care: Taking care of yourself is essential for sustaining your creativity and passion. Make sure to prioritize self-care activities such as exercise, meditation, or spending time with loved ones. Taking breaks when you need them and avoiding overexertion will prevent burnout and help you maintain a sustainable podcasting journey.

5. Build a supportive network: Surround yourself with like-minded individuals who understand the challenges of podcasting. Join online communities, attend conferences or events, and connect with fellow

podcasters. Building a network of supportive peers can provide valuable advice, inspiration, and motivation to keep going when times get tough.

6. Be open to evolving: The podcasting landscape is constantly evolving, and it's important to adapt and embrace change. Stay informed about industry trends and be open to experimenting with new formats or topics. Embracing change and staying flexible will help you stay relevant and sustain your podcasting journey for the long term.

Finding the balance between ambition and sustainability in podcasting is a continual process. It requires self-awareness, adaptability, and a willingness to reassess and adjust your goals and strategies. By setting realistic goals, prioritizing quality, practicing self-care, and building a supportive network, you can find the sweet spot that allows you to pursue your podcasting ambitions while maintaining a sustainable and enjoyable podcasting journey.

Remember, it's not about being the biggest or most popular podcast, but rather about creating meaningful content that resonates with your audience and brings you joy. Find that balance, stay true to your passion, and your podcast will flourish in the long run.

Implementing Best Practices for Long-term Podcast Growth

Implementing best practices for long-term podcast

growth is essential for maintaining a successful and thriving podcast. While it's easy to get caught up in the excitement of launching your podcast and gaining initial traction, it's important to have a plan in place for long-term growth and sustainability. In this section, we will discuss some key strategies and practices that can help you take your podcast to the next level and ensure its continued success.

1. Consistency is key: One of the most important factors in podcast growth is maintaining a consistent release schedule. Whether you choose to release new episodes weekly, bi-weekly, or monthly, it's crucial to establish a routine and stick to it. Consistency builds trust and loyalty with your audience, as they will come to expect and look forward to new episodes from you. Make sure to plan ahead and have a backlog of episodes ready to go, so you can stay on track even during busy times.

2. Quality content is paramount: While consistency is important, it should never come at the expense of quality. Your podcast's success ultimately relies on delivering valuable and engaging content that resonates with your audience. Take the time to research and prepare your episodes thoroughly, ensuring that you're providing unique and insightful perspectives on your chosen topic. Invest in good equipment and audio editing to ensure a professional listening experience for your audience. By consistently delivering high-quality content, you will attract new

listeners and keep them coming back for more.

3. Understand your target audience: To effectively grow your podcast, it's crucial to understand who your target audience is and what they want to hear. Conduct market research, analyze listener feedback, and engage with your audience to gain insights into their preferences and interests. This will help you tailor your content to meet their needs and provide them with value. Regularly reassess your target audience and adjust your content strategy accordingly to stay relevant and continue to attract new listeners.

4. Leverage social media and other marketing channels: In today's digital age, social media and online marketing are powerful tools for podcast growth. Establish a strong presence on platforms that are popular among your target audience, such as Instagram, TikTok, X, or Facebook. Regularly engage with your followers, share updates about new episodes, and provide behind-the-scenes content to build a community around your podcast. Consider collaborations with other podcasters or influencers in your niche to expand your reach. Additionally, leverage email marketing, guest appearances on other podcasts, and cross-promotion to reach new listeners.

5. Optimize your podcast for discoverability: Ensuring that your podcast can be easily discovered by new listeners is essential for growth. Use relevant keywords in your episode titles, descriptions, and show notes to

improve search engine optimization (SEO). Submit your podcast to directories and platforms such as Apple Podcasts, Spotify, Google Podcasts, and Stitcher to reach a wider audience. Encourage your existing listeners to leave reviews and ratings, as positive reviews can boost your podcast's visibility and credibility.

6. Continuously learn and improve: Podcasting is an ever-evolving medium, and it's important to stay up to date with industry trends and developments. Take the time to listen to other podcasts in your niche, attend conferences or webinars, and participate in online communities to learn from fellow podcasters. Continuously seek feedback from your audience and be open to constructive criticism. Use this feedback to refine your content, delivery, and overall podcasting strategy to improve and grow.

By implementing these best practices, you can lay a strong foundation for long-term podcast growth. Remember, building a successful podcast takes time, dedication, and ongoing effort. Stay consistent, provide valuable content, understand your audience, leverage marketing channels, optimize for discoverability, and continuously learn and improve. With these strategies in place, your podcast will have the potential to thrive and reach new heights.

15 What's New in Podcasting for 2025: The Future of Audio Content

As we dive into 2025, the podcasting industry is embracing innovation and change with open arms. From AI-driven content creation to immersive audio experiences and interactive formats, the future of podcasting is rich with possibilities. For podcasters, this means new tools and opportunities to engage with audiences in creative ways. For listeners, it means a more dynamic, personalized, and immersive audio experience.

AI-Enhanced Content Creation

Artificial Intelligence is making waves in podcasting, not just in terms of production but also in content creation. AI tools can now assist in generating episode outlines, suggest engaging topics, and even craft compelling scripts. For podcasters, this means more efficient content creation and the ability to tap into new ideas and trends with ease. Additionally, AI-driven voice synthesis can create lifelike audio, allowing for diverse and dynamic guest appearances without requiring everyone to be physically present.

Immersive Audio Experiences

The evolution of audio technology has given rise to immersive audio experiences. Spatial audio, which creates a 3D sound experience, is becoming more prevalent in podcasts. This technology allows listeners to feel like they're in the midst of the action, enhancing storytelling and making podcasts more engaging. Imagine a true crime podcast where you can hear the nuances of a crime scene or a nature podcast where you're enveloped in the sounds of a rainforest.

Interactive Podcasts

Podcasts are no longer a passive experience. Interactive podcasts are gaining traction, enabling listeners to influence the content in real-time. Features like live polls, Q&A sessions, and interactive storylines allow audiences to shape the direction of episodes. This not only increases engagement but also fosters a deeper connection between podcasters and their listeners.

Decentralized Podcast Platforms

Decentralization is changing the way podcasts are distributed and monetized. Blockchain technology is being leveraged to create decentralized podcast platforms, where content creators have more control over their distribution and revenue. This shift offers greater transparency and fairness, allowing podcasters to bypass traditional gatekeepers and engage directly with their audience.

Enhanced Personalization

Personalization is at the forefront of podcasting advancements. Algorithms are becoming more sophisticated, providing listeners with highly curated recommendations based on their preferences and listening history. This means you'll discover new podcasts that are perfectly tailored to your interests, making your listening experience more enjoyable and relevant.

Podcasting and Augmented Reality

Augmented Reality (AR) is making its way into podcasting, offering a new layer of interactivity. AR can enhance podcast content by overlaying visual elements onto the real world. For example, a podcast about historical events could include AR visuals that bring historical sites to life in your living room. This fusion of audio and visual elements creates a richer, more immersive experience.

Micro-Podcasting and Short-Form Content

As attention spans shorten, micro-podcasts and short-form content are on the rise. These bite-sized episodes, often ranging from a few minutes to around ten minutes, cater to listeners who want quick, digestible content. This format is perfect for delivering brief updates, quick tips, or succinct stories, fitting neatly into busy lifestyles.

Enhanced Monetization Options

Podcast monetization continues to evolve, with new revenue streams emerging. Beyond traditional advertising and sponsorships, podcasters are exploring direct listener support through subscription models, exclusive content, and crowdfunding. Integration with e-commerce platforms is also growing, allowing podcasters to seamlessly promote and sell products related to their content.

Increased Focus on Accessibility

Accessibility in podcasting is becoming a priority, with more creators focusing on making their content available to everyone. Features like automated transcripts, multilingual support, and enhanced audio descriptions are becoming standard practice. This ensures that podcasts are accessible to individuals with disabilities and non-native speakers, broadening the reach and impact of podcast content.

Cross-Media Integration

Podcasting is increasingly integrating with other media formats. Cross-media projects that blend podcasts with video content, books, and even live events are becoming more common. This multi-platform approach allows podcasters to reach audiences across different mediums and create a more cohesive and immersive brand experience.

Appendix

Launching your Podcast Journey: Essential Resources and Tools

First and foremost, you'll need a reliable microphone. The quality of your audio is crucial in podcasting, and investing in a good microphone will make a world of difference. There are several options to choose from, ranging from USB microphones to XLR microphones. Do your research and find one that fits your budget and recording setup.

Next, you'll need recording and editing software. Audacity is a popular and free option for editing your podcast episodes. It's user-friendly and offers a wide range of features to enhance your audio quality. If you're looking for a more professional option, Adobe Audition and GarageBand are great choices.

In addition to recording and editing software, you'll also need a reliable hosting platform for your podcast. A hosting platform allows you to upload your episodes and distribute them to various podcast directories, such as Apple Podcasts and Spotify. Popular hosting platforms include Libsyn, Podbean, and Anchor. Consider the features and pricing options of each platform before making your decision.

Once you have your recording equipment and hosting

platform set up, it's time to create a captivating podcast cover art. Your cover art is the first impression listeners will have of your podcast, so make sure it's eye-catching and represents your brand or podcast theme. Canva is a user-friendly graphic design tool that offers templates and customizable elements to help you create stunning cover art.

In addition to cover art, you'll also need a podcast website. A website serves as a central hub for your podcast, where listeners can find information about your show, browse episode archives, and access show notes. WordPress and Squarespace are popular website builders that offer podcast-specific themes and plugins to make the process easy.

To attract listeners and promote your podcast, social media platforms are a must. Create accounts on platforms like TikTok, X, Instagram, and Facebook, and start sharing engaging content related to your podcast. Engage with your audience, collaborate with other podcasters, and use hashtags relevant to your niche to increase your reach.

To ensure your podcast reaches a wide audience, it's important to submit your podcast to various podcast directories. The most popular directory is Apple Podcasts, followed by Spotify and Google Podcasts. Each directory has its own submission process, so make sure to follow their guidelines for a seamless submission.

Lastly, don't forget to invest in some good headphones. While not technically a necessity, headphones will help you listen closely to your recordings, identify any issues, and make necessary edits. Look for headphones that offer good sound quality and comfort for long editing sessions.

Get Ready to Roll: Your Comprehensive Podcasting Checklist

To ensure a smooth and successful launch, it's important to have a comprehensive podcasting checklist that covers all the key elements. In this section, we'll provide you with a step-by-step guide to help you get ready to roll.

1. Define Your Podcast Niche and Format:

Start by clearly defining your podcast niche and format. What is your podcast about? Who is your target audience? Will it be an interview-style show, a narrative storytelling podcast, or a solo talk format? Understanding your niche and format will guide your content creation and help you attract the right audience.

2. Create a Content Calendar:

Developing a content calendar is essential for staying organized and consistent with your podcast episodes. Decide on a regular release schedule, whether it's weekly, biweekly, or monthly, and plan out your episode topics in advance. This will ensure that you have a steady stream of content and prevent last-minute scrambling.

3. Prepare Show Notes and Episode Outlines:

Show notes provide a summary of your podcast

episode, including key talking points and links to any resources mentioned. Take the time to prepare show notes and episode outlines for each episode. This will not only help you stay focused during recording but also make it easier for your audience to follow along and refer back to specific information.

4. Script or Outline Your Episodes:

Decide whether you want to script your episodes word-for-word or use an outline to guide your discussions. While scripting can help ensure a polished and structured episode, using an outline allows for more flexibility and a conversational tone. Choose the approach that aligns with your podcasting style and make sure to practice before hitting record.

5. Set Up a Professional Recording Space:

Find a quiet space in your home or office where you can record without interruptions or background noise. Consider investing in soundproofing materials, such as foam panels or a portable vocal booth, to improve the acoustics. Test your recording setup, including your microphone and recording software, to ensure optimal audio quality.

6. Create a Consistent Branding Identity:

Develop a consistent branding identity for your podcast across all platforms. This includes designing a captivating logo, choosing a color scheme, and creating visually appealing cover art. Carry this branding through to your podcast website and social media profiles to establish a recognizable and professional image.

7. Write Compelling Episode Titles and Descriptions:

Craft attention-grabbing episode titles and descriptions that entice your audience to listen. The title should be concise, yet descriptive, while the description provides a teaser of what to expect in the episode. Think of them as mini-marketing tools to attract potential listeners and improve discoverability.

8. Practice Recording and Editing:

Before officially launching your podcast, spend some time practicing your recording and editing skills. Get comfortable with your microphone and recording software, and experiment with different editing techniques. Practice makes perfect, so don't be afraid to redo episodes until you're satisfied with the final result.

9. Develop a Marketing and Promotion Strategy:

A successful podcast relies on effective marketing and promotion. Outline a strategy to increase your podcast's visibility, such as utilizing social media platforms, collaborating with other podcasters, or reaching out to relevant communities and influencers. Consider running ads, guesting on other podcasts, or participating in industry events to expand your reach.

10. Launch and Submit to Podcast Directories:

Once you're ready to share your podcast with the world, it's time to officially launch. Upload your episodes to your chosen hosting platform and submit your podcast to popular directories like Apple Podcasts, Spotify, and Google Podcasts. Follow their submission guidelines and make sure your podcast meets their requirements for a smooth approval process.

By following this comprehensive podcasting checklist, you'll be well-prepared to launch your podcast with confidence. Remember, consistency, quality content, and effective promotion are key to building and growing your podcast audience.

Demystifying the Lingo: A Handy Glossary of Podcasting Terms

1. Bitrate: Bitrate refers to the amount of data processed or transmitted per unit of time in your podcast audio. It determines the audio quality and file size. A higher bitrate generally means better audio quality but larger file sizes. Common bitrates for podcasts range from 64kbps to 192kbps, depending on your preference and hosting platform limitations.

2. Show Notes: Show notes are written summaries or outlines of your podcast episodes. They provide listeners with additional information, links, and references related to the episode's content. Show notes are essential for engaging your audience, improving search engine optimization (SEO), and making it easier for listeners to find and reference specific topics discussed in the episode.

3. Intro and Outro: The intro is the opening segment of your podcast that introduces the show, sets the tone, and captures the audience's attention. It typically includes the podcast name, host introduction, and a brief overview of what the episode will cover. The outro is the closing segment that concludes the episode, includes any call-to-action or promotional content, and provides a memorable sign-off.

4. RSS Feed: RSS (Really Simple Syndication) is a format used to publish regularly updated content, such